# Love and Sex Are Not Enough

# Love and Sex Are Not Enough

Charles P. De Santo

Introduction by John M. Drescher
Foreword by Anthony Campolo

HERALD PRESS
Scottdale, Pennsylvania
Kitchener, Ontario

Except where otherwise noted:
New Testament quotations are from *Good News for Modern Man* (TEV) Copyright © by American Bible Society, 1966, 1971. Used by permission.
Old Testament quotations are from the Revised Standard Version of the Bible, copyrighted 1946, 1952, © 1971, 1973.

LOVE AND SEX ARE NOT ENOUGH
Copyright © 1977, by Herald Press, Scottdale, Pa. 15383
  Published simultaneously in Canada by Herald Press
  Kitchener, Ont. N2G 4M5
Library of Congress Catalog Card Number: 76-45731
International Standard Book Number: 0-8361-1809-X
Printed in the United States of America
Design: Alice B. Shetler

10 9 8 7 6 5 4 3

Dedicated
to the loving memory
of my parents

# CONTENTS

*Author's Preface* ........................... 9
*Introduction by John M. Drescher* ......... 11
*Foreword by Anthony Campolo* ........... 13
*Prologue* ................................. 17
1. Christians in a Pluralistic Society ......... 21
2. The Relevance of Christian Faith
   to Life and Marriage .................. 30
3. The Importance of Family Background .... 38
4. The Impact of Youth Culture ............ 46
5. The Pros and Cons of Early Marriage ..... 54
6. Love Is Not Enough .................... 62
7. Sex Is Not Enough ..................... 74
8. Principles of Mate Selection ............. 90
9. Rational Courtship ..................... 116
10. Summary and Conclusion .............. 134
*Appendix: Mating in the Faith, by Levi Miller* 141
*Notes* .................................. 147
*General Index* ........................... 151
*Index of Scripture References* ............. 158
*The Author* ............................. 159

## AUTHOR'S PREFACE

This book was written as one Christian's response to much of what is being advocated and propagated in contemporary popular literature for youth consumption. No one would deny that beliefs and values have radically changed over the past decade. In no area is this more true than in the realm of heterosexual relations—dating, mate selection, and courtship. While there is no progress without change, all change is certainly not progress in the positive sense. No doubt the "latest" discoveries in science and technology are generally for the betterment of humankind (although many would question that). It does not necessarily follow that what is in vogue or currently being practiced among men and women in heterosexual relationships is an improvement.

As Christians our point of reference is Jesus Christ and the basic principles which He enunciated. Our ethical and behavioral standards must always be based upon the Word and will of God as revealed in the Scriptures. Our concern is not only "What is good for me as an individual?" but also "What is good for the family, the community, and the nation?" Furthermore, our concern is with the consequences of our behavior in the long run as well as the short run. My hope as author is that this book will provoke young people, especially Christian young people, to think more seriously about the entire dating, mate selection, and courtship process.

I would like to thank the following people for their assistance: Dr. E. Luke Matz for his careful, critical reading of the book, and the many suggestions he gave which enabled me to clarify some important concepts; Mark Sundburg and Mrs. Bea Heid for their reading and suggestions for improvement; Norma A. De Santo, my good wife, for suggesting numerous grammatical and stylistic changes; Paul M. Schrock, book editor of Herald Press, for his editorial assistance in preparing the manuscript for publication; John M. Drescher for his Introduction; and finally, Dr. Anthony Campolo, for writing the Foreword.

August, 1976 *Charles P. De Santo*
Lock Haven State College
Lock Haven, Pennsylvania

## INTRODUCTION

While many books promote current fads and ideas about dating, courtship, and marriage, De Santo selects and shares many of the enduring qualities and guidelines which have stood the test of time. The author blends a strong biblical stance with sound sociological and psychological understandings. After all, the God who made us is concerned with the whole person and has laid down abiding principles which are basic to our being. The author has tested his concepts in the classroom and in his counseling.

Charles De Santo is clearly committed to the Christian faith and unashamedly speaks from this perspective, while he also shares a variety of differing viewpoints in the areas he discusses.

If one is looking for much that is new, he will not find it in this volume. If one is seeking clear, concrete, and dependable guidance on dating, courtship, and mate selection brought together in a single volume he will discover that a great deal is offered here.

This book will serve as a helpful resource for discussions with young people in a variety of settings. It will be useful as a text for courses in marriage and the family. Youth leaders, Sunday school teachers, pastors, and parents will find much in *Love and Sex Are Not Enough* which will clarify what is needed for a solid marriage relationship. The content of this book is not mere theory. Its discussion of basic essentials is backed up by many generations of happy homes.

Some will see this book as quite conservative. However, I believe we live in a day when many parents, spiritual leaders, and youth are looking for such a volume. The new morality, rapidly changing standards (or lack of standards), and the emphasis on relativism have clearly demonstrated that they do not hold the key to happy, spiritually fulfilling, lifelong marriages. We need clearer guidance and firmer ground than these offer.

*Love and Sex Are Not Enough* reminds us not to confuse American and Western cultural concepts and practices with Christianity. They are far from synonymous. We need to be grounded in Christ and guided by proven values and principles. We need to remember that we live in a society with competing value systems and that much of what is commonly accepted today is faulty at the very foundations. Present practices in dating, courtship, and mate selection seem increasingly to lead to a breakdown of happy marriage and family life.

The further I read in *Love and Sex Are Not Enough*, the more I felt the need of such a book. I am persuaded that many others are waiting for such an approach. A deeper understanding and practice of the basics treated in this volume is overdue.

*John M. Drescher*, Author
*Meditations for the Newly Married*
Scottdale, Pennsylvania

# FOREWORD

The destabilization of marriage in the modern world is a reality with which we must deal. More than 25 percent of marriages contracted in the United States at present will end in divorce. Add to this the fifteen to twenty percent more marriages which will end in separation without the benefits of a legal divorce, and you have the shocking reality that between forty percent and fifty percent of all marriages in America will be dissolved.

Of the marriages that do remain intact, a significant proportion experience such serious unhappiness that the partners would get out of them if they could. The reasons such unhappy persons do not leave marriage are too numerous to list, but they include the convenience of the marital arrangement, social pressures, and religious values. According to one estimate, only thirty-five percent of marriages measure up to the expectations for happiness which the participants who entered into them had imagined. In short, marriage is a failing institution.

Sociologists have analyzed the disintegration of this institution. Their insights are worthwhile and their studies shed tremendous light on what is taking place and why it is occurring. However, sociology is a value-free science. The representatives of this discipline will not prescribe what should be done to remedy the conditions which have become alarming to those of us who view the family as a religiously legitimated institution and who view marriage as a sacred contract. Sociologists simply analyze, explain, and predict; they do not suggest. Yet, in the midst of the confusing society in which we live, we look for informed prescriptions that would remedy what many of us feel has become a social sickness. We need the information that sociologists provide if we are to reconstruct a family that is stable in our society. But we need more than that.

At the turn of the century about 70 percent of Americans were living in rural, agrarian settings. Only 30 percent were living in what might be called metropolitan areas. Through rapid industrialization and urbanization, all of this has changed. Today, 70 percent of the population live in metropolitan areas; only 30 percent live in rural settings, and less than 5 percent of the American population are engaged in farming. These figures are significant because family life, as we have known it, is very functional for people who live on farms. Large families are economic assets in a farm economy. Marriage is stable because wives and husbands are economic partners in the farm venture.

As people move off the farms those economic factors which have contributed to the family oriented lifestyle cease to play important roles. In the urban setting, marriage is not basically an economic arrangement but a romantic episode. Children in the urban setting are not economic assets but become economic liabilities. When it costs $40,000 to raise a child in today's society, it is no wonder that couples are planning smaller families.

Urban society does not provide a function fit for the traditional agrarian family. The question is, can marriage be restructured and redefined for the urban world so as to insure its survival without eroding the biblical imperatives which those in the Judeo-Christian tradition feel to be important?

Those of us who are committed to the Judeo-Christian tradition believe that marriage is divinely ordained. Furthermore, we believe that the Scripture is a source of practical guidance for persons who want to make a success of marriage. Unfortunately, people who are steeped in biblical knowledge are often unaware of the insights of social scientists. Hence, we are caught in a situation where sociologists often understand the problems but don't know the answers, while those who have a faith commitment often have answers but do not grasp the problems. Charles De Santo offers a refreshing exception to this dilemma. Combining sociological information with biblical insights, he offers enlightened views on how marriage and family life can be saved.

> *Anthony Campolo,* Chairperson
> Department of Sociology
> Eastern College, St. Davids, Pennsylvania
> **Visiting Lecturer,** University of Pennsylvania

# PROLOGUE

If you landed in the United States from Mars, or if you came here from one of the traditional societies of Europe or Asia which has *not* been influenced by the mass media, or films exported from Hollywood, you would probably think that our dating, courting, and mate selection system was completely irrational. As a friend from India said in one of my college marriage and family classes: "You Americans marry for 'love.' Then you end up hating each other and getting divorced!" Why is it that what seems so rational to us—marrying for "love"—appears so irrational and foolish to visitors? Are they wrong, or could it be that since we have been so brainwashed by our culture, we are unable to see how dysfunctional our system really is for establishing stable, productive marriages?

In our mass media (television, movies, popular magazines), as well as in our educational system, the emphasis is upon individualism, freedom, and hedonism or pleasure. Furthermore, we are led to believe that love is all that matters, and that "sex" is the greatest expression of love. It is my contention that *love and sex are not enough* for a stable, happy marriage. A marriage must be based on more than that—at least for Christians.

## 18/Love and Sex Are Not Enough

Romantic love is rooted in emotional attraction and it has an air of mystery and wonder about it. It is associated with infatuation, sensuousness, and physical appeal. Often, "love" is a cover for mere physical desire or lust, but because it seems too crass to admit that one would like to have sex with a person, he uses the euphemism "love." That is supposed to make everything okay. But the Christian cannot be satisfied with such a limited definition of love. Love includes more than the concept of romantic love. In addition, the Christian's conscience will not permit him to use love as a mask for physical desire. For the Christian, love is best defined by the Apostle Paul in First Corinthians: "Love is patient and kind: love is not jealous, or conceited, or proud; love is not ill-mannered, or selfish, or irritable; love does not keep a record of wrongs; love is not happy with evil, but is happy with the truth. Love never gives up: its faith, hope, and patience never fail. Love is eternal."[1]

The Greek word which Paul uses for love is *agape*, the self-giving type of love that God demonstrated when he gave Himself in Christ to redeem us. As the Apostle John said: "We love because God first loved us."[2] Because we have been loved by God, we are obliged to love our "brother" and "sister"—non-Christian, as well as Christian.[3] Furthermore, our Lord commanded us, "You must love your fellowman as yourself."[4] Therefore, since Christians are expected to love everyone, love, per se, is not a sufficient reason for marriage.

Neither is sexual desire alone a good and sufficient reason to marry. Sex, for the Christian, cannot be experienced or discussed in a vacuum. It is an expression of the "self" or personality; we are sexual beings. How we express ourselves physically toward members of the opposite sex is not only a good indicator of our own self-image, but also the valuation we place upon members of the opposite sex.

As Christians we believe that the sexual act is basically a spiritual act of communion that we express through the medium of physical intercourse. Since God has made us so that virtually any two human beings of the opposite sex can relate to each other physically, there must be more to marriage than sex.

Therefore, it is my thesis that dating, courtship, and mate selection must be based upon more than "love" and "sex." As Christians we repudiate the extreme and distorted emphasis that our society places upon romantic love and sex, as well as upon freedom, individualism, and hedonism. We are committed to Jesus Christ and are members of His body, the church. We are not free to do as *we* please, but only to do as *He* pleases—to live in a vital relationship with the whole body of Christ and our fellowman. Personal pleasure is not our goal—especially if it in any way injures another human being. Our standards are not "relative," that is, subjectively defined by the desires we have in a given situation. We are committed to the absolute standards of God revealed in the Holy Scriptures and in the life and teachings of Jesus Christ.

I set forth in this book a Christian perspective on dating, courtship, and mate selection. To a non-Christian my views will undoubtedly appear radically different when placed against the background of secular thought that pervades our society, but to a committed Christian, I think they will appear sound, rational, and biblical. God gave us minds to use, and this includes using them in the area of male-female relations.

I ask only that the reader stay with me until the end of the book before passing judgment on the validity of my theses. Also, I would like to ask that what I have to say be evaluated in the light of the Bible and Christian principles. It is important that we do not confuse American or Western culture with Christianity. They are far from being the same. Nor are middle-class values, or any other "class" values for that matter, synonymous with Christian values.

# 1

## Christians in a Pluralistic Society

The United States is a noble experiment in that it has such a diverse population. Virtually every race and nationality, as well as every major religious faith, intermingle within the borders of the United States and Canada. This is what we mean when we say that our society is a pluralistic one. We not only have Protestants, Catholics, and Jews, but we have Muslims, Hindus, Buddhists, not to mention those committed to humanism, secularism, scientism, agnosticism, and atheism. In addition there are religious surrogates such as communism and nationalism. Almost all of these groups are "evangelistic" in the sense that they have adherents who seek to convert others to their faith.

Since we are committed to a philosophy of government that advocates freedom of worship, as well as freedom of speech and of the press, we would not have it any other way. This means, however, that we must be aware of the various systems of belief that compete for our allegiance. If we are to be effective and fruitful Christians in today's world, we must not only know our own faith, but also something about the competing systems of belief.

Since we live in a pluralistic society, we do not have a single culture to which all subscribe 100 percent. While there is a set of values and beliefs to which all of us more or less subscribe, there are also many subcultures that are peculiar to individual ethnic, racial, and religious groups. As Christians we belong to one of these subcultures. For good or for ill, it is not too different from the dominant culture in our society. Some would suggest that we should really constitute a counterculture, since Western culture is largely non-Christian, if not pagan. Nonetheless, the wide diversity of subcultures associated with the various nationalities (e.g., Italian, Jewish, Polish, Puerto Rican, black, Japanese, American Indian, Chicano, etc.) does constitute unique or contrasting lifestyles. Furthermore, the unique values of each group are often associated with one of the religious faiths. These differences have important implications for mate selection, as we shall see later.

## Christianity and Religious Pluralism

At the risk of oversimplifying the complexity of our society, I would suggest that the religious faiths can be divided into three groups—Christian, theistic, and secular. The Christian group includes over 250 Protestant denominations and the various branches of the Catholic

Church. The second group includes the Jewish faith and some Eastern religions, while the third group includes a large number of people who adhere to religious surrogates. The latter have a faith that they live by, but it does not include the worship of a deity. In this category I would include those who not only worship science, some political ideology, or materialism, but also those who have made a *god* of food, clothing, sex, pleasure, or themselves. Since most contemporary idolaters do not erect images that are normally associated with idol worship, we are often not aware of the wide diversity of religious faiths within our borders.

The fundamental difference between Christianity and the major competing faiths is that we are committed to the belief that we can have a vital relationship with God in the person of Jesus Christ, and that He has given us an objective standard to live by—the principles set forth in the Holy Scriptures. We do not philosophize about whether God exists or not, or whether there are sound ethical principles to guide us in life. We begin with the belief that God does exist and that He has revealed in the Bible all that we need to know to live a full, meaningful, and useful life.

The major competing faith today, if we exclude political ideologies, is what I would call *relativistic secularism*. This modern version of intellectual or practical atheism rejects not only God and the notion that He has given us a special revelation of His will and purposes for us in Scripture, but it maintains that there are no absolutes to live by except "the absolute" that says: "It all depends on how *I* look at it, or how *I* feel about it." According to this faith the individual and his desires and his happiness are the most important thing![1] If it gives *me* satisfaction and it does not harm others, then the behavior is okay. Usually, however, the merits of the behavior are based upon the short-range consequences and not the long-range ones. Often the individual does not take into consideration whether or not the act will adversely affect the family, community, and/or the larger society. Subjectivism—"how *I* perceive it"—is the primary consideration and motivation for action.

The Christian, however, cannot forget that he belongs to God who has redeemed him in Christ, and that he is obligated to love God with all his heart, soul, mind, and strength, *and* his neighbor as himself. He is not only a member of his biological family, but also a member of the larger family of God. He is not his own: he has been bought with a price.[2]

It is important to be aware of the fact that everyone has some frame of reference, that is, some group with common values (peer, family, and/or others) from which he takes his cues for behavior. These values and beliefs that form the basis of behavior of the various groups rest upon assumptions that cannot be proved. As Christians, we also operate from basic assumptions. We assume the existence of God and we accept by faith the validity of the gospel and the truthfulness of Scripture. This is not to say that there is no solid historical and archaeological evidence for what we believe. There is. Ultimately, however, it is a matter of faith. My point is that everyone, consciously or unconsciously, subscribes to some basic assumptions by which he lives. Therefore it is not a question of whether one will be religious or not; *all men are religious*. Man is incurably religious. As Voltaire said: "If God did not exist, it would be necessary to invent Him." This is indeed what many have done, invented deities. The question is, however, "Can man-made deities make an individual whole?"

## Christianity, Relativism, and Absolutes

A characteristic of our age is its emphasis on relativism, the popular notion that what is right and good is determined by the individual in a given situation, apart from any objective standard. It is worth noting that many sociologists and anthropologists would not agree. While beliefs and behavior are relative, they are always relative to a given culture with a coherent set of values. Cultural traits do not hang suspended in midair. Whether a given behavior pattern is acceptable or not does not only depend upon how *I* look at it or how *I* feel about it. It depends on how my society looks at it! It all depends upon how my reference group or subculture looks at it, and how they feel about it, if I want to feel good about it.

Furthermore, there are cultural universals to which all societies subscribe. All societies have a family system with rules regulating sexual behavior and marriage, ownership of property, general morality, status, and the like. While these universals are interpreted differently by various societies, nonetheless everyone in each society has a sense of right and wrong. C. S. Lewis makes the point that the very fact that man is conscious of right and wrong, suggests the existence of a Mind or a Deity who impinges upon us. If this were not the case, how is it that we are bothered by the notion that there is something wrong with our world?

But we still have to answer the question: "Is truth relative?" The answer is yes and no. The answer is yes if we are speaking in a sociological sense. Traits vary from culture to culture. A trait that is taboo in one society, may be prized in another. For example, polygamy is acceptable to a Muslim, but it is unacceptable to the Christian. Still another example would be the difference between the attitude of the Mennonites and other denominations toward war. Mennonites are pacifists, while Presbyterians, Lutherans, Roman Catholics and numerous others generally are not. Whether one is a pacifist or not depends on the subculture in which one was reared, since it is part of the total culture complex of one's religious community. But whether pacifism or nonpacifism is "right" is not relative.

Let me give still another example of cultural relativity. My mother, who was born and reared as a child in southern Italy, believed that you could give someone "the evil eye!" Southern Italians believed that if they looked at an individual a certain way and pronounced a curse upon him, the victim would suffer some misfortune. It actually worked. However, when Italians came to America in the early twentieth century they found that "the evil eye" did not work on Anglo-Saxons—it did not fit into our culture complex. Therefore, a sense of right and wrong is relative to a given culture, but this does not mean that because a society subscribes to a particular belief it is necessarily true.

While there is truth in the notion that "if men define situations as real, they are real in their consequences," nonetheless, mere belief does not make a belief true. No amount of belief will make the world flat or turn the moon into green cheese. As Christians we believe that truth is eternal and that it is found by rigorous and disciplined study. All truth ultimately finds its unity in God and Christ. All cultural traits must be tested by the principles set forth in the Scriptures. If the Bible does not forbid a practice by "letter" or "spirit," then it is a matter of conscience and personal preference. But if a cultural practice or belief is contrary to the teachings of Scripture, then it is not true. We would say, therefore, that *the truth* is not relative, but it is relevant; all cultural traits must be judged by it.

### *The Christian, Ethnocentrism, and Prejudice*

Christians, then, live in a pluralistic society in which there are many competing faiths, each with its own values, each a separate subculture, each seeking in one way or another to attract others to it. When we take a stand and say, "I am a Christian," and refuse to identify and/or socialize through dating with non-Christians, we may be accused of being ethnocentric and prejudiced. If we define ethnocentricism as the tendency for a people to think that its own subculture (values, beliefs, and practices) is better than others, then Christians could be accused of being ethnocentric. For we do believe that our faith is the true faith and that by responding positively to the offer of God's love and forgiveness in Jesus Christ we have become the reconciled children of God. We stand in this special relationship, however, not because we are any better than anyone else, but because we have accepted God's reconciling grace extended to us in Jesus Christ. We are sinners, too, but we have accepted God's offer of forgiveness. We have been called to service by Christ and we have committed our lives to God in Christ.

If being a member of the body of Christ and a member of a unique subculture means that we are to be labeled ethnocentric—then so be it. We would hardly be Christians if we did not believe that Jesus Christ was "the way, the truth, and the life."[3] When we reflect upon the attitudes of those around us, there are few individuals who do not believe that their religion or philosophy of life is the best for them. However, Christians would not deny others the right to subscribe to their philosophy of life. We are committed to freedom of choice. As we would not want others to dictate to us or coerce us to subscribe to a particular faith or ideology, so we would not deny this freedom to others. We believe everyone should have the right to choose his own faith and philosophy of life.

While Christians might be accused of being ethnocentric, I do not believe it is legitimate to do so. Nor is it legitimate to call us prejudiced if we only date other Christians. When we say that a person is prejudiced, we are speaking about negative attitudes or feelings toward members of a particular minority group. Christians do not believe that any race or ethnic group is intrinsically inferior or superior to another. We are all children of God and potentially brothers in Christ. But we must distinguish between social and civil rights. If I choose to restrict my dating to Christians, this is my social right. The Bible tells us to identify with other believers, and not to be unequally yoked together with unbelievers.[4] Therefore, if we choose to date only Christians we should not be accused of discriminating in the negative sense, but in the positive sense. Just as members of other religious and ethnic groups believe that it is the better part of wisdom to select as a marriage partner one from their own religious and/or ethnic group, so do Christians. We are not prejudiced, but merely obeying a tenet of our faith.

As Christians, therefore, we are aware that we live in a pluralistic society with many competing subcultures, each having its own value system. We do not look to secular literature for guidance in matters of faith and morals. Our basic source is the Scriptures and the teachings of Jesus Christ which serve as our guide in interpersonal relations—including dating, courtship, and mate selection. Before we turn to the business of male-female relationships, however, let us look at the Christian faith as a basis for a viable lifestyle. It is my contention that the foundation for a meaningful relationship within courtship and marriage must begin with a solid commitment to Jesus Christ. To this we now turn our attention.

# 2

# The Relevance of Christian Faith to Life and Marriage

Most young people wrestle with the question of identity, "Just who am I?" If we are to relate meaningfully to others we must understand who we are. Only then can we begin to interact meaningfully with others.

### The Christian Faith, Briefly Considered

When we begin to discuss the Christian philosophy or way of life, we can begin either with God or man. Personally I like to begin with God as revealed in Scripture because there we learn what He is like, as well as what He expects of us. Traditionally the Christian community has insisted that since God created us in His image and for fellowship with Himself, as well as with our fellowman, we can only be at peace with ourselves and others after we have been reconciled to God. Indeed, our

*The Relevance of Christian Faith/31*

Lord summed up the commandments when He said: "The Lord our God is the only Lord. You must love the Lord your God with all your heart, with all your soul, with all your mind, and with all your strength.... You must love your fellowman as yourself. There is no other commandment more important than these two."[1]

When we begin to think about God, we immediately become aware that we have not measured up to His expectations for us. We feel like Isaiah the prophet who, when he got a glimpse of the majesty and holiness of God in the temple at Jerusalem, said: "Woe is me! For I am lost; for I am a man of unclean lips, and I dwell in the midst of a people of unclean lips; for my eyes have seen the King, the Lord of hosts!"[2] The Apostle Peter had a similar experience in the presence of Jesus the Christ. When he sensed that Jesus was the Holy One of God, he said to him: "Go away from me, Lord! I am a sinful man!"[3] Therefore, while we begin with God, we are almost immediately compelled to examine ourselves because of a new sense of self-awareness.

The Bible makes it clear that we are self-centered, sinful beings who have fallen far short of God's standard of righteousness. We are not only egocentric, but this egocentricity manifests itself in all of our dealings with others. Now this is an important point, not only theologically, but also socially. Theologically, I am acknowledging that as a sinful, self-centered human being I need to repent and ask God's forgiveness, and the forgiveness of others whom I have wronged. I need to be reconciled with God and man. Sociologically speaking, it means that I am willing to accept the fact that I am a finite creature—one who lacks knowledge, has a tendency to make wrong judgments, and frequently offends others by word and deed. I am saying that I am not sufficient in and of myself. I need the help, the insight, and the forgiveness of others, as well as of God. It is difficult to relate to persons who are unwilling to admit that they are *not* omniscient. Such individuals are convinced that they are totally right, refusing even to listen to other points of view. It is almost impossible to relate to *perfect* people.

The Christian faith teaches that when we come to see God as the Holy One, we accept ourselves as sinful beings who need God's forgiveness. He offers us this forgiveness through the person and work of Jesus Christ.[4] God in Christ makes us whole and enables us to stand on our own two feet.[5] As He extends grace and power to us, so He enables us to extend grace and forgiveness to others.[6] The question of finding forgiveness and extending it to others is crucial in interpersonal relations.

The Apostle Paul cautions us that we are not to think of ourselves more highly than we ought to think.[7] We are to keep constantly before us the fact that we are sinners who have been saved, not by our own works of righteousness, but by the vicarious death of Jesus Christ. This ought to keep us humble and malleable in interpersonal relations, especially within marriage. Since as individuals we do not bring perfection into the marriage relationship, we ought not to expect it from our spouses.

Conversion to God through faith in Christ is essential because it enables us to see ourselves as we truly are—sinners in need of the mercy of God. Now it is at the time we come to realize that God has accepted us in Jesus Christ that we can come to accept and respect ourselves—yes, even love ourselves. Because we admit that we have offended both God and our neighbor, and because we accept the fact that God in Christ has forgiven us, we need no longer pretend. We can be ourselves. We can draw upon the power of God's Spirit as we strive to become new creations in Christ Jesus. We can reach out and love our neighbor as we love ourselves!

### *The Christian Faith, Foundation for a Workable Marriage Relationship*

As Christians, then, our basic commitment is to God—to "glorify Him and to serve Him forever." And how do we serve Him? We serve Him not only by worshiping Him and maintaining some kind of a devotional life that will enable us to grow in the knowledge of His will and purposes for us, but also by reaching out in service to others—all mankind. If we give our primary allegiance to God in Christ, then any human relationship that we establish will be on a solid footing, including our relationships to members of the opposite sex. Why? Because both of us will be sharing a common faith with a common goal in life. We could diagram it this way:

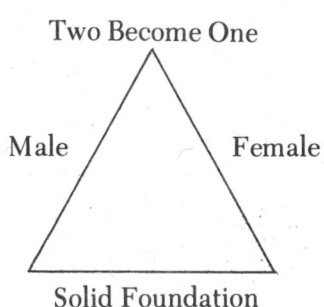

Two Become One

Male  Female

Solid Foundation
Common Faith in God Through Christ

Since both share the same faith, problems that arise will not shake the foundations of the relationship because both are building upon the solid foundation of Jesus Christ.[8]

On the other hand, if a couple does not build upon a common faith in Christ they are more apt to falter when the problems and the circumstances of life overwhelm them.

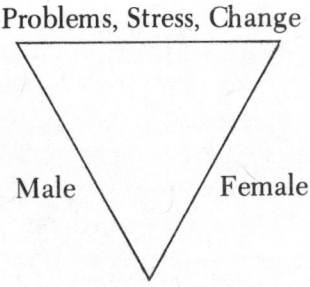

It seems to me, therefore, that rather than Christianity not being relevant, as some maintain, it is both relevant and essential to an honest, vital marriage relationship. In fact, Christianity provides positive guidelines for both marriage and the family.

1. *Christians are urged to marry Christians, not unbelievers.* In this way the couple share a common commitment to values that both of them can support and work to achieve.[9]

2. *Christians marry for life.* Our Lord said that a man and a woman leave their father and their mother and the two of them become one. Nothing is to separate them. This is the ideal. This lifetime commitment is important

because the couple enter the marriage expecting to resolve their differences and problems, using conflict as a means of growth, and not as an excuse for separation and/or divorce.[10] While divorce is permitted within the faith, the reasons for resorting to it are limited.

3. *Christian love is an ideal toward which a couple strive.* While full maturity in our expression of love is never achieved in this life, nonetheless our Lord challenges us to seek to achieve it. It is a goal that, by the grace of God, we can grow into—a oneness of purpose in Christ's service.[11]

4. *Humility is the mark of the Christian.* If both truly are humble and submissive to one another, their interpersonal relations will not be fraught with continual friction.[12]

5. *Prayer is the means by which both keep in touch with God's will and purpose for their lives.* Prayer, together with the reading of the Word of God, is the means by which our spiritual lives are nurtured. Both disciplines will increase their understanding, mutual respect, and consideration of one another.[13]

6. *Forgiveness is an integral part of the married experience.* We are not to end the day unreconciled to each other. Indeed, marriage vows might best read, "Love, honor, and forgive!" As suggested earlier, Christians are realistic about human nature. We admit that we are sinful. In fact, the closer we live to God, the more conscious we will become of our own sinfulness. Because of willfullness, ignorance, and self-centeredness, we are bound to offend by word, attitude, and behavior. The Christian couple will readily repent, ask forgiveness, and seek reconciliation. Just as God in Christ has forgiven us,

so we must forgive those who offend us.[14]

7. *Christians believe that sexual love is ordained of God and that it is an effective means of communication and communion.* We are enjoined by Scripture to share through sexual intercourse regularly. To refuse sex, except under special circumstances, is to reject one's spouse—it is a sin.[15]

8. *Husbands and wives are equal before God.* There is no superior and inferior status, merely a difference in familial roles. The husband is to assume the role of leader within the marriage.[16]

9. *Finally, Christians participate in the life of a church.* Active involvement within a church is a vital part of Christian growth. Since Christian love must be demonstrated, the Christian willingly identifies with others of like faith in service to and for other believers, as well as to those in need outside of the fellowship of the church. To refuse to participate because one believes that there are hypocrites in the church is to raise oneself above his brother or sister, and to succumb to the sin of pride and self-righteousness. The believing community was ordained by Christ, and we are admonished in Scripture to worship corporately and to serve in it.[17]

These are but a few of the principles and concepts of Christianity which serve as a viable guide for interaction both inside and outside of marriage. Students who are familiar with the Bible are aware that all of the teachings of the prophets, Christ, and the apostles are invaluable for Christian growth. The Christian faith is relevant to all life's needs including the issues one faces in choosing a marriage partner and in living together as husband and wife.

Any couple who share a fundamental commitment to Jesus Christ is indeed fortunate. While problems and conflicts are a part of human existence, faith in God's power and Word offers strength and guidance for every circumstance in life.

# 3

# The Importance of Family Background

*The Process of Socialization*

An important concept that is often minimized and neglected in books dealing with courtship is that of *socialization*. By socialization we mean that lifelong process by which we acquire the values, beliefs, attitudes, and behavior patterns of our culture. You might ask, "What does this have to do with dating, courtship, and mate selection?" My response is that it has much more to do with it than "love" and "sex" because we are largely a product of our family, church, and community interaction. We did not just appear on the scene as a young adult. We were nurtured by, and we interacted with, a host of "others."

As a result of the intimate interaction with individuals in primary groups, such as family, peer groups at school, church, and neighborhood, we acquired values we presently hold. While we were not conscious of the fact that we were being socialized, nonetheless the process was going on. Values, for the most part, are *caught*, much more than they are taught. Although formal instruction does play a significant part in the formulation of our life and world view, our family environment undoubtedly makes the greatest impact upon us.

*The Family, Primary Agent of Socialization*

We are socialized, then, into a specific subculture, namely, our own family subculture. In a pluralistic society such as ours, various ethnic groups have lifestyles which are unique in addition to the values that they share with other Americans. As children reared in an Anglo-Saxon, Italian, German, Irish, Puerto Rican, or black family, we have unconsciously absorbed the beliefs and traditions of our subculture.

In addition to being born into a given ethnic subculture, we are also born into a specific socioeconomic class. Although we do not think of our society as a stratified one, we need to be aware that we do indeed live in a society which has class divisions. While we do not have rigid class lines, we are born into one of the three broad categories—lower class, middle class, or upper class. Sociologists generally agree that an individual in a specific class, regardless of ethnic background, has more in common with people who occupy the same stratum he does than he does with someone of another class within his own ethnic group. This is important to keep in mind when we think about dating and mate selection. If we date someone in the same socioeconomic class and/or with the same ethnic background, we can assume that we have much more in common than when there is a significant mix of races, ethnics, classes, and/or religions. By this I mean that we do not have to stop to explain what we mean by something we say or do, since both of us share similar subcultures.

Within our families, our parents instruct us formally and informally, and by this process of interaction we acquire our values and beliefs. This process begins when we are mere infants. If our home is a friendly place permeated with love and understanding, we sense the world to be a friendly place and we develop an optimistic, positive attitude toward life. Our parents' values, which they internalized largely from their own families and from experiences with significant others, are the ones that they have shared with us, and we in turn have internalized them and we will probably share them with our children. As we mature we internalize these values. Our attitudes and beliefs regarding Christ and the church, members of other races, education, work, recreation, and the like are usually absorbed as a result of familial experiences at home.

Generally speaking, it is from our parents that we learn either to be kind, considerate, and understanding, or to be sarcastic, inconsiderate, and intolerant. We learn also that "problems" can be solved in either a rational or an irrational manner. We can solve them by rational discussion, or we can leave them unresolved by becoming loud and aggressive, or by remaining silent, or by slamming the door in a fit of anger and rushing out of the house. The home is the place where our characters and personalities are, for the most part, molded.

## The Importance of Family Background/41

*We Are Active Participants in the Socialization Process*

I do not want to give the impression that we are passive in this socializing process. Just as our parents' interaction with us conditions the type of response we give to them, so our words and actions affect their attitude and response to us. This is one explanation for the differences between children within a given family. Our personalities are not only the product of heredity, but to a large extent they are the product of the sum total of our interactions both inside the family, as well as outside. As we age, our personalities are constantly growing and changing as a result of our interaction with others, which steadily increases. When we reach adolescence, especially the latter part, we must assume the major responsibility for our personal growth, both spiritual and psychological.

We cannot, as so many in our society attempt to do, blame personality defects and deficiencies on our poor home or neighborhood environment. As Ezekiel the prophet said, children cannot excuse themselves of their sins and faults by saying that their "fathers have eaten sour grapes," and as a consequence their teeth have been set on edge.[1] Each individual is responsible for his own behavior, vices as well as virtues. In other words, no one compels us to do anything. Within certain limits, we have the power and the freedom to choose, and we must assume the responsibility for our behavior and its consequences. We cannot blame others.

Furthermore, it is important to remember one of the basic tenets of the Christian faith—that all of us are sinners. There is no such thing as a sinless person. Therefore, since families are composed of individuals, it logically follows that families will have to grapple with problems and conflicts which will inevitably arise because of the sinfulness and the shortcomings of each member of the family. Just as we as individuals must seek to grow in the grace of Christ, so our parents, along with the individual members of the family, must strive to grow in Christ. This is a lifetime process. If we do not like some of the traits that we have acquired within our family subculture, it is up to us to seek to change them.

### We Can Be "Born Again" or Resocialized

One of the basic facts of the gospel, clearly demonstrated by countless men and women through the centuries, is that an individual can be "born again."[2] If one accepts God's offer of forgiveness in Jesus Christ and commits his life to Him, his life will be gradually turned around. He will become a new creation in Christ Jesus through what we might call the spiritual process of *resocialization* as the mind is transformed.[3] This transformation, however, takes place over a lifetime—it is a gradual one. When one becomes a Christian he still has the same innate intelligence, he is still a "Yankee" or a "Rebel," he is still a member of his ethnic group, he is still a member of a particular stratum within society, and he is still a member of the same family subculture. While he will doubtlessly experience great changes in attitude, disposition, and sense of stewardship as he changes from an egocentric person to a Christ-centered person, a great deal about his life will remain the same.

How much one changes after conversion depends upon the quality of his life prior to profession of faith. Obviously, one who was reared within a Christian home and did not particularly rebel against his socialization into Christian values will not undergo as dramatic a change as someone who did rebel or one who did not have the advantage of being reared in a Christian home. Furthermore, the amount of change that takes place is related to the opportunities one has in life. While the potential for growth and change is always present, the course it takes depends upon how open one is to the leading of the Spirit, as well as to how obedient he is. By the grace of God we can overcome a besetting sin or weakness, but it will take much work and prayer.[4] For the most part, however, we tend to continue in the behavior patterns we acquired within our family subculture, including our unique religious community.

### Denominations Are Subcultures, Too

As Christians we have been reared in various denominations and churches. These represent subcultures within American culture, as do our family and ethnic groups. Mennonites are different from Methodists, just as Presbyterians are different from Pentecostals. The doctrines and practices that we have internalized over eighteen or more years of our lives within our denominations are a vital part of us. A person is hardly aware of how Baptist he is, for example, until he attends an Episcopal church service with all of its formal ritual and liturgy. On the other hand, one may not realize how much he has internalized the quiet reverence of his church service until he attends a free Pentecostal service where reverence is not necessarily associated with quietness. For his part, the Pentecostal would describe the formality of most church services as "cold," with no manifestation of the Spirit.

The point that I am making is that there are not only ethnic subcultures, and socioeconomic subcultures, but there are also denominational subcultures within the Christian church. These do not dissolve or evaporate into thin air because one says, "Oh, but we love each other!" The power of culture to mold and shape us cannot be overemphasized. Paul was aware of this when he said to the Christians at Rome, "Don't let the world around you squeeze you into its own mold."[5] He wrote this in the first century before there was even a hint of the mass media that we wrestle with today! When considering persons to date seriously—dates who may become marriage partners—it is best not to get involved with those with sharp religious-and cultural differences.

*We Are Socialized into a Racial and Ethnic Subculture*

In addition to being socialized into a unique family, ethnic, and religious subculture a word should be said here about racial subcultures and socioeconomic class. Racial and ethnic groups have unique subcultures, although there are many similarities between racial groups within the United States. Tastes in food, music, dress, as well as behavior patterns vary in these groups as they do from one socioeconomic class and region of our country to another. These interlocking endogamous factors are all part of our cultural heritage which is transmitted to us through the process of socialization. While there probably are greater differences between classes than there are between races, nonetheless, the differences between races can be quite significant. More will be said about that later.

A good exercise for anyone serious about his courtship is to sit down and write a brief sociological analysis of his family. In this family socio-autobiography include the values and beliefs that your family has shared with you, as well as an analysis of how the various members of the family played their roles (mother, wife, father, husband, and children). If both the young man and the young lady will do this, then they can begin to explore areas which might constitute problems later.

From our observations regarding the importance of the socialization process in personality and value formation, let us now turn to a consideration of youth culture.

# 4

# The Impact of Youth Culture

*Adolescence, a Recent "Invention"*

One of the important phenomena of today is the existence of an age-span called "adolescence." Adolescent young people with the help and manipulation of business and industry, have developed their own culture, or subculture. Undoubtedly young people have heard their parents say, "When I was your age we didn't have a hi-fi, a car, leisure time, and the spending money that you kids have today!" If this was true of the parents of youth today, it is even more true of their grandparents. It is difficult for teenagers to realize that when their parents or grandparents were children there was no such thing as a jet plane, space travel, television, and certainly not the great number of telephones and automobiles that we have today. The world has never before experienced the rapid technological and scientific developments that have made mass production possible, nor has the affluence they have produced ever been shared by all classes of people as it has been in the Western world.

The presence of so many material amenities which we all enjoy and take for granted are largely the product of the past seventy-five years. Alvin Toffler, in *Future Shock*, divides the history of the world into lifetimes of sixty-two years each, totaling 800. He says: "Of these 800, fully 650 were spent in caves. Only during the last seventy lifetimes has it been possible to communicate effectively from one lifetime to another—as writing made it possible to do. Only during the last six lifetimes did masses of men ever see a printed word. Only during the last four has it been possible to measure time with any precision. Only in the last two has anyone anywhere used an electric motor. And the overwhelming majority of all the material goods we use in daily life today have been developed within the present, the 800th, lifetime."[1] Little wonder that he suggests that many persons today suffer from "future shock"—the inability to adjust to the rapid change taking place in our society. The emphasis today is indeed upon change, newness, and the future. No sooner is something marketed than the manufacturer is updating the product and issuing a "new and improved" version of it. All of this is related to adolescence and youth culture, but how?

We said that adolescence is a recent creation, and it is. It is a product of the industrial revolution, more particularly of the twentieth century—especially since World War II. Let me illustrate. When my mother emigrated from Italy to the United States as a child of eleven, she never lived through an adolescent period, that is, a period of eight to ten years after puberty devoted largely to play and education. She worked in a factory *over* forty hours a week until she was sixteen, when she married! This was the experience of many Americans at the turn of the century. They passed directly from childhood into adulthood. There was no compulsory education then, and if there was, it certainly was not enforced.

Following World War I, and especially after World War II, as we became increasingly urbanized and industrialized, we no longer needed the mass of unskilled labor we previously did. This meant two things: (1) we had to provide young people with verbal, math, and vocational skills needed to fill positions demanded by industry; and, (2) we had to keep young people occupied and out of the labor market because there were not enough jobs to go around. Also, as families moved off the farms into the cities, children were no longer economic assets. This meant that family size began to decline, so that today families are smaller than they have been since the depression of the thirties. Therefore, as we have moved from an industrial society into a postindustrial one (a society in which over half of the workforce is engaged in service activities and not production), the period of adolescence has steadily increased. As a result of these changes, the period of adolescence for those who remain students may extend to age twenty-five.

We see, then, that economic factors have produced not only adolescence, but also affluence. Mass production has made it possible for virtually all Canadians and Americans to enjoy the gadgetry that we have come to believe essential for the "good life." Most young people today are no longer compelled or permitted to work. Instead they engage themselves during these years in an extended period of education that will prepare them for positions in our automated society. All is not work, however, since much of their time is spent in recreational and consumer activities of one kind or another in our "fun" culture. Never in history have young people had so much discretionary money at their disposal.

### Characteristics of the Youth Subculture

The young people who occupy this time-span have their own values which are reflected in their subculture. I prefer the term *subculture* to youth culture because the values that youth hold are largely those of the dominant culture in our society—they are not unique to their age group.[2] Youth merely carry to an extreme the values espoused by their parents. But what are the values that young people have chosen to emphasize and intensify, or more accurately, the values that Madison Avenue has sold them?

Certainly one of their values is *living for the present*. For the most part, the mass media emphasizes, "Do it, now!" "Go right out and buy it—don't wait another minute!" "Charge it!" "Fly now, pay later!" We have infected our youth with a virus which one might identify as *Nowism*. Many adults are infected, also. Indeed it is considered unpatriotic not to buy, do, think, or say it NOW.

A second value is *hedonism or pleasure*, largely sensuous pleasure. We live in a permissive age—one in which anything goes. We have moved from a paternalistic attitude toward our young people to a totally permissive one. We have moved on most campuses from standing in the place of parents to a complete abdication of responsibility for the social and moral welfare of our young people. With reference to the mass media, we have also swung to an extremely permissive position. Both television and the motion picture industry, not to mention the popular press, are saturated with love triangles, quadrangles, *ad nausea*, as well as with violence of every kind. Wine, women or men, and song are thought to be the equivalent of the "good life." Young people today live in a fun culture. While a small minority are reared to assume responsibility and to work while attending school or college, most live in a make-believe world that bears little resemblance to the work world they eventually must enter.

*Individualism* is a third value of youth. Whereas our grandparents lived in a familial society that took seriously the needs and wishes of others in the family and in industry, today's youth subculture emphasizes freedom and individualism. "Do your own thing." "Hang loose." "Don't hassle me!" "That's not the way I see it!" "Bug off!" "Let it all hang out!" These expressions and others reflect the sentiment of many young people within our society today.

Finally, our society and our youth prize youth itself, as well as *newness*. The business of making wigs, falsies of every description, cosmetics for men and women, and designing clothes is booming. We have no old people in our society—only shades of youth! But this emphasis on the "new" is deceptive and destructive because many have insisted that morality must also change as well as fashion, science, and technology.

*Basic Christian Values Do Not Change*

Since most would agree that what is new in science, medicine, and technology is quite often better than what existed previously, many have been duped into thinking that what is new in morality is also better. Hence, we hear young people and adults, teachers in high school as well as in college and university, propagating permissiveness under the rubric of the "new humanism." What Christians have always called "selfishness," "irresponsibility," and "immorality," is now being labeled "the new morality."

The truth of the matter is that while science and technology do become outdated and obsolete, basic Judeo-Christian standards of morality do not. The basic needs of man have remained the same. The old tried and true ethical principles of Christianity are still valid, and they are needed today as much as they ever were in the past. We know enough about past history and enough time has elapsed in our lifetime to know that the moral permissiveness of our society (experimental communes, key clubs, wife swapping, and the like) have brought anything but the happiness their advocates have promised or desired.

While I have said that these are some of the values of the subculture of contemporary secular youth, too often they are also the values of Christian youth and adults. Peer pressure and the influence of our mass society are not a phenomenon of one age group. All age groups are manipulated by the mass media until they almost believe that it is their obligation to buy the latest fashion in thought, as well as material things. As Christians we must constantly renew our minds—purging them of the worldly desires of the flesh and the mind that our society would foist upon us.[3]

Christian young people who are aware of the shortcomings of the contemporary secular youth subculture, as well as the pressure of the mass media and mass society, should try to avoid the "generation gap." The principles of Christ are not for youth or adults. They are for all. It is important that young people associate with peers who espouse the same Christian values that they and their parents subscribe to. I am not suggesting for a moment that the social interests of adolescents and adults are or should be the same. I cannot appreciate some of my children's music anymore than they can appreciate some of mine. Nor do I want to be with young people all the time—we are at different stages in the life cycle and our interests and needs are different. But what I am saying is that basic Christian values are relevant to each age group and we must integrate them into our lives. They must become the basis for our behavior.

Christian parents and young people ought to do all within their power to keep the lines of communication open. If we have difficulty, we should talk about it—try to iron out the problem. If we cannot talk it out with our parents, then we should locate a trustworthy adult friend with whom to talk things over. Most pastors, church officers, youth leaders, some schoolteachers, and school counselors are more than willing to help. As we shall see later, one of the positive correlates of a happy marriage is parental approval. For this reason, among others, we should always strive to keep the channels of communication open.

Many young people who feel that they cannot relate to

their parents try to remedy the situation by entering into an early marriage. While this may seem like an easy way out, for most it only compounds their frustration and misery. Let us now turn to a consideration of the pros and cons of early marriage.

# 5

## The Pros and Cons of Early Marriage

Since Christian young people are a part of the main stream of society, they cannot help but be "infected" with the pervasive emphasis upon sex and romantic love. Many of their peers are not only getting engaged at seventeen, eighteen, or nineteen, but they are also getting married. It is estimated that more than one third of the "first-time brides" in recent years in the United States have been teenagers.[1] While it is true that most early marriages occur among young people within the lower socioeconomic stratum of society, it is not uncommon for middle-class youth to marry early, also.

Christian young people naturally wonder about the wisdom of taking such a significant step so early in life. Just why do some marry so young? What are the advantages and disadvantages, not only for the individual, but also for his family and society? Can one realize God's best for himself or herself by marrying early? These and many other questions inevitably come to mind, and they are worthy of serious consideration.

### Reasons Often Given for an Early Marriage

There are several reasons young people give for marrying early. A few of them are good, but most of them are not so good. *One common reason is to escape a bad home situation.* Either the parents are constantly arguing and bickering, or the conflict involves both parents and children. At any rate, whatever the cause of the conflict within the home, one may feel that he can escape from a bad home situation through an early marriage. The unfortunate thing is that we can seldom escape from a bad home situation because we ourselves are usually a part of it and it has become a part of us. We are a part of the conflict situation. We absorb the behavior patterns of our family and we bring these into our new marriage. The ways our parents talk, act, and react to problem situations have usually become an integral part of our personality structure and, unless we are aware of this, we cannot begin to change.

Sociologists note that children from unhappy homes tend to have unhappy marriages themselves. This is often true because the socialization process, which was largely an unconscious experience, is nonetheless a very real one. A Christian young person who lives in a conflict-ridden situation ought not to panic and seek what appears to be an easy way out. The wiser course of action is to try to be a peacemaker within the home, while at the same time attempting to develop one's own personality in accordance with Christian principles. If one feels that the situation is critical, he can talk to his pastor who may suggest additional ways of working at the problem. Several other good sources of help are the local mental health clinic, the high school counselor, or a youth leader in your church or community in whom you have confidence. Usually ministers, counselors, and other mature friends are more than willing to help, and they will keep your problems confidential.

*A second reason given for an early marriage is sex*. The couple believes that they are in love, and they want to marry so that they can consummate their love for one another through sexual intercourse. Now on the surface this sounds logical—at least they have said that they believe that sex is something that belongs within the bonds of marriage. But are they ready for all the responsibilities that go with marriage? There is much more to marriage than sex! While the stated goal is happiness through sexual union in marriage, there are many aspects of marriage which they may not have taken into consideration.

Young people who plan an early marriage ought to ask themselves the following questions: Are we economically self-sufficient? Are we mature enough emotionally to handle the problems and pressures that will come our way? Where will we live? Have we actually sat down and computed what it will cost to run a home? If we need to live with one set of in-laws, will we have the social, physical, and psychic privacy we need? Will we be able to finish our education, or will marriage frustrate or terminate any career plans? Once young people begin to raise such questions, and talk things over with their

## The Pros and Cons of Early Marriage/57

parents and mature relatives, many more questions and issues will surface.

Young people who marry for "love" and "sexual" satisfaction usually find that the unanticipated or latent consequences of marriage are so numerous that the sexual satisfaction they anticipated never materializes. Sexual intercourse is really one of the physical ways we express a social relationship. It does not occur in a vacuum. It is affected by the totality of married relationships. Furthermore, sex, even with love, is not sufficient "glue" to bind two people together.

*Rebellion against one's family is a third reason for early marriage*, although it may not be a conscious one. Rebelliousness usually is associated with conflict in the home. Marrying early, or marrying someone of whom our parents do not approve, can be an attempt to punish them. The young person, in effect, is saying, "I'll show them. I'll just go ahead and get married!" When this is the reason for marriage both parent and child are shortchanged. Certainly parents are hurt when their children do rash things that bring pain and hardships upon themselves and others, but the real loser is the boy or the girl.

As a Christian the answer is not vengeance. The things that are causing one to rebel need to be worked out. Probably both parties need help, but if one's parents will not seek counseling, at least the young person can improve the situation by the insight he will gain.

*A fourth reason for early marriage, which also is often an unconscious one, is a desire to achieve adult status and recognition.* In our society a girl of seventeen who is married is called "a young married woman"—not a girl.

Likewise the boy is now "a married man." Teenage friends and young adults who are still students are regarded as *non*adults—even if they are twenty-five. But if a couple are not emotionally, economically, and socially mature, the ritual of marriage will not change them—it is not a magic rite. Most teenagers are still quite tied to their parents and are not ready for marriage.

*A fifth reason for marrying early is that young people may feel lonely in a society that seems to be growing increasingly impersonal.* They are out of high school, working at a job, and desire companionship. If the couple have been going together for a reasonable period of time (hopefully at least a couple years), if one or both have good jobs with an adequate income, if both are emotionally mature, and if they have the blessings of their parents, then it may be reasonable to marry. However, in a fun culture in which the roles played by young people are only a fraction of those enacted within the family, it is never wise to rush into marriage. If one is lonely and desires companionship, these needs can be satisfied within the family, a peer group, an organization, or a youth fellowship. Furthermore, we must be careful lest the loneliness be a neurotic condition. If it is, it is better to seek counseling and overcome the problem than to marry and find that the loneliness still persists. Marriage does not change the personality. We must be able to give, as well as receive, affection and support in marriage. Unless we can, the relationship will be strained and one-sided at best.

*Finally young people often marry early because the girl becomes pregnant.* Shotgun weddings are quite common among adolescents. But is pregnancy sufficient

## The Pros and Cons of Early Marriage/59

reason for marriage? If, on the one hand, the couple know each other well, are in love and like each other, and if they were anticipating marriage later, this is one thing. But if, on the other hand, the girl became pregnant after having intercourse with someone whom she scarcely knew, and they realize they are not suited for each other, it may be unwise to compound the situation with marriage. Two wrongs do not make a right.

Wouldn't it be better either to put the child out for adoption, or to keep the baby and raise him within the family? If the girl keeps the baby, eventually she will probably meet someone whom she truly respects and who will be the kind of husband and father she and the child need.

### Reasons for Not Marrying Early

Probably the reader has gathered by now that I do not see much advantage in marrying early. Let me suggest some reasons why I have not encouraged early marriage.

1. *Early marriage interferes with career development for both sexes.* The world has changed drastically since the days of our grandparents and parents. The extended family has given way to the nuclear family. The nuclear family of just husband, wife, and children (if the couple has any) does not provide the traditional supports for family members. Individual resources and governmental social services must be used to compensate for the functions the extended family supplied. Therefore, it is essential that we prepare for and obtain the best positions possible, given the talents we have.

Furthermore, with the emphasis on sexual equality in the social and economic spheres, it is also important that women have an opportunity to develop their skills in a career of their choosing. Early marriage cuts short career development for both spouses.

While we can find statistics to support the fact that married college students do better than those who are single, the statistics do not include those who have dropped out of college and cut short their schooling because of marriage and/or pregnancy.

2. *Not only are careers cut short, but personality and intellectual development are often arrested.* When we drop out of high school, vocational school, or college, we also find that our time is taken up by the job and the concerns of the family. We miss out on the reading, the bull sessions with peers, the opportunity to travel, and the like, that enable liberally educated young people to enjoy life to a greater degree. This may also limit their usefulness to God and society.

3. *Before we settle down to one individual for life it is a good idea to associate freely with many young people.* In this way we not only mutually benefit from the social interaction, but we have the opportunity to learn about different types of individuals. After we are satisfied that "the grass is not greener on the other side," then we are ready to settle down. Of course there are exceptions. Some young people marry a high school friend whom they have known for years, but these are the exception rather than the rule.

4. *Finally, as a Christian, we ought to strive to achieve our highest potential in every way.* By the time we get to the last two years of high school or into college we have some idea where our talents or abilities lie. We must resist settling for second or third best merely because our

peers are marrying, or because we feel the pressure from within or without for sexual gratification.

One of the best things a young person can do is to write out a philosophy of life, including not only one's expectations regarding sexual behavior, but also career goals. Just what does one hope to accomplish in the next five to ten years? How would marriage hinder or facilitate these goals? By placing some of these things on paper, and by discussing them with peers and parents, a young person can hammer out a positive, constructive Christian life and world view.

Early marriage? For a few it may work out, but it seems to me the better part of wisdom is to wait until the apron strings have been completely severed, and one has established his own identity. The fact that over half of the marriages that take place before age nineteen end in divorce, should tell us something!

# 6

## Love Is Not Enough

When I ask my students to define "love," I usually get a response something like this, "You can't define love, it's too personal! It means different things to different people." Some add, "Love is an emotion and cannot be defined." But if I ask, "Who of you was 'in love' once, but is now no longer 'in love' with that person?" several raise their hands. Then I ask, "Now tell me, why is it you no longer 'love' that person?" What usually follows is an enumeration of attitudes, beliefs, and practices that they did not like.

If we can tell what makes us stop loving someone, then we ought to be able to give specific reasons why we love him or her. I believe that love can be defined fairly precisely, and that we can know what we mean when we say that we love someone.

### Four Greek Words for Love

Love is indeed a complex term that means different things to different people in various relationships. The Greek language has several more precise words for love than we do in English. Let's consider four of them.

*Eros* usually has a physical, sensual, and sexual connotation.[1] It is basically egocentric or self-centered. It is the kind of love that seeks to possess and enjoy the object of affection. Robert K. Kelley says: "We might define *eros* as a sensual desire that recognizes no limits of propriety or custom."[2]

*Philia* denotes social love, the kind that one demonstrates for a friend. It is devoid of sexual connotation. It is friendship based upon shared interests.[3]

*Storge* denotes family affection. Love of parent for child and child for parent. It is the kind of love that is open and accepting.

*Agape* refers more to the will than to the emotion, and it conveys the idea of showing love by action. It is a self-giving love—love that gives even when the other does not merit it. God's love is the best example; His love for us was demonstrated in the giving of His Son to redeem us. Kelley relates *agape* to marriage, saying: "Such love is a necessity if two persons are to maintain a permanent and harmonious relationship. In this kind of love there is a willingness to give when the loved one is not able to reciprocate, whether it be because of illness, failure, or simply an hour of weakness. It is a love that can repair bonds severed by unfaithfulness, indifference, or jealousy. . . . Such love does not do away with eros [or *storge* and *philia*] but rather transforms it into its highest and finest fulfillment."[4]

Now it seems to me that when we speak of love for someone of the opposite sex, heterosexual love, we need to include all four basic concepts. We need the *agape* as the basic component because there needs to be a commitment. We need to be able to empathize, to give understanding, and to identify with the other person. We need to be able to "hang in there" when support is needed, whether we find any satisfaction or not. This certainly is the example of divine love we get from the Scriptures. God loves us all the time—when we are obedient to Him, as well as when we are wretched and in need of His love the most.

Then, too, we need *philia*, the companionate relationship—friendship. This might better be conveyed by the word "like." The people we like are those who share our values—those with whom we can generally identify. Through social interaction we find great comfort and support. *Philia*, coupled with *storge*, the open accepting affection characteristic of familial relationships, needs to be mixed with *agape*.

Lastly, *eros* introduces the emotional aspect of heterosexual love. We find satisfaction in the limited bodily contact we have before marriage—just being in his or her presence. In marriage, however, *eros* plays a vital part; physical love becomes one of the means of communicating our total feeling of oneness. These four words include the basic ingredients of heterosexual love.

### Infatuation and Romantic Love

"How do I know when I have fallen in love?" "What are the telltale signs?" These are questions we probably all ask at one time or another. First of all, we need to clarify one thing. We do not "fall in love." What is often described as "falling in love" is nothing less than infatuation. By infatuation we mean being physically attracted or "turned on" by someone of the opposite sex—but this is *not* love.

Robert O. Blood says: "An affair based on sexual attraction to the exclusion of companionship and care is infatuation."[5] Infatuation is a false love. If it were true love, it would include other elements such as care or concern, respect, responsibility, and knowledge. Erich Fromm believes these elements to be essential to mature love.[6] This is not to say that infatuation is necessarily wrong, but it certainly cannot be construed to be love. Infatuation may lead us to date someone, however, and then the relationship may grow into mature love.

Furthermore, love is not something we "fall into" and "out of." It is something that "we stand in"—it is a "state of being." Fromm suggests that either we are a loving person or we are not. Jesus tells us that we must love our neighbors as ourselves. When we are reconciled to God through faith in Jesus Christ, when we accept God's offer of forgiveness, then we find it easier to accept ourselves. We understand that all love comes from God and that we are to be channels of His love. As children of the God of love, we are enabled to love everyone. By virtue of our standing in His love, we love.[7] Therefore, we do not fall in and out of love—it is a state of being from which we reach out to others.

We must not only distinguish between infatuation and mature love, but we must also distinguish between infatuation and romantic love. Historically, romantic love has been associated with the medieval period and the age of chivalry. It is believed that romantic love originated when knights sought to woo ladies married to other men. Their relationship was filled with excitement, daring, and mystery as they sought to win the hearts of these ladies of the court and manor. While this clearly was an emotional, exciting, and sensuous affair, theoretically it stopped short of sexual intercourse. This romantic concept evolved further in subsequent centuries and blended with that of married love. Americans, and especially Hollywood, have developed the idea of romantic love more fully than any other people.

However, romantic love has been present throughout history. Secular literature, as well as the Old Testament and apocryphal books, make numerous references to it. Ira L. Reiss cites the work of anthropologists who witness to the fact that romantic love is found in many non-Western societies among primitive tribes.[8] Romantic love then, was, and is a rather common phenomenon, but the unique thing about our society is that we have been "taken in" by it. My Taiwanese colleague in sociology says that Asians regard romantic love with great suspicion and distrust. They see it as a pseudo-love which blinds individuals or narrows their field of perception so that they fail to consider the more weightier matters related to courtship—the cultural, socioeconomic, and familial factors.

To be infatuated or romantically attracted to someone of the opposite sex does not mean we are "in love," at least not from a Christian perspective. While our culture tells us that we are in love when we can't sleep, have butterflies in our stomach, lose weight, and the like, from a rational Christian perspective this is not enough.

Romantic love is not mature love. This is not to say that there is no place for romance in courtship and marriage. An element of emotion, physical attraction, and idealization are probably a part of most successful courtships and marriages in our society. If these elements become excessive, however, there is no real foundation upon which to build a secure, solid marriage relationship.

### *"Like" Versus "Love"*

At this point it might be helpful to look at some of the characteristics of mature love. Before we do this, however, I would like to make one of my theses clear: love, per se, is neither a good nor a sufficient reason for going steady or for getting married. *As Christians we are expected to love everyone.* This is not only a command of Christ; it is a prerequisite for being truly human. It is my contention that when we reach the marriageable age (late adolescence and early adulthood), we should select from among our friends and acquaintances someone whom we would like to get to know more intimately. When we find such a person it should be someone we *like*. We can know that we *like* this person if we share similar values, beliefs, interests, and life-goals. While we must love everyone, in the sense that we wish them well, we cannot possibly *like* everyone. There are some individuals that I love, but I do not particularly like them. I choose not to socialize with them on an intimate basis. I pray for them and wish them God's best, but since we have virtually nothing in common and our personalities clash, we do not spend much time together. We would utterly bore each other if we had to spend several hours together.

It is possible for two people to be physically attracted to each other (infatuated or romantically in love), and yet not really *like* each other. This is one factor contributing to the breakup of many young people who are dating or courting. They become involved physically early, and then after having sex together, they dissolve the relationship. There was no *liking* there, nor was there a mature love for the other person. While they used the language of romantic love, it was in reality *lust*. Excessive sexual desire, lust, often leads to sexual exploitation under the guise and euphemism of "love."

Mature love, therefore, when related to heterosexual interaction, courtship, and marriage, must include the elements of *like* and *personal compatibility*. By the latter I mean there must be a mesh, a sense of oneness, harmony, and the ability to communicate openly most of the time. Robert O. Blood, Jr., defines the compatible couple as one whose intrinsic characteristics fit together in a mutually beneficial manner.[9] If the personalities mesh, if the couple *like* each other, then this can lead to mature love. But to *liking*, personal compatibility, and mature love, there must be added similarity of cultural and socioeconomic background. We shall discuss this at length in the chapter on mate selection.

## Characteristics of Mature Love

So far we have said that infatuation and romantic love are not mature love. We said that love alone is not a sufficient basis for either courtship or marriage. Now I would like to return to defining further what I mean by mature love by looking at some definitions others have offered. William M. Kephart refines a definition of romantic love to include: "(1) a strong emotional attachment toward a person of the opposite sex; (2) the tendency to think of this person in an idealized manner; and (3) a marked physical attraction the fulfillment of which is reckoned in terms of touch."[10] Since this definition stops short of any discussion of married love, I find it unacceptable for our purposes here, although it is an excellent definition of romantic love.

Robert Blood offers another definition of love. He defines heterosexual love as "an intense emotional attachment between two people of the opposite sex."[11] While intensity may vary, he says that it is more intense than mere friendship. "The emotionality of love signifies its dynamic characteristic." Since *attraction* may not be reciprocal, Blood prefers the word *attachment.* He says that "attachment is a better word than attraction because it symbolizes the solidarity of the relationship between two partners." But, he adds, that since attachment can be too close there also needs to be *release.* "Release is an expression of trust, respect, and acceptance" which permits each individual the freedom to grow.[12] Furthermore, he says that love is a blend of at least four things: "sexual attraction, companionship, care, and affirmation." He sees sexual attraction and companionship as an integral part of caring and commitment. Otherwise the first two can be exploited.

Kelley says that mature love includes at least three elements: (1) a mutual sense of personal worth and respect, (2) the ability and willingness to empathize, and (3) a sense of commitment to the other person—the will to succeed. "Mature love is the kind of love that does not change with the seasons or with changing circumstances, but accepts life both at its best and at its worst."[13] Kelley disagrees with Freud who suggests that the basic drives are sexual in nature and that these control our love. For Kelley the basic element in love is psychological/spiritual, and he believes that this should control and regulate the sex drive.[14] With this interpretation I am in hearty agreement.

Fromm insists that individuals are either loving persons or they are not. As loving persons, our love should include the elements of caring, responsibility, respect, and knowledge. He maintains that these take time to develop. Love is not something that we turn on or off, but it is a state of being. We are not born loving; it is an art that we must cultivate. The Christian would add that we learn best how to love by imitating the love of God revealed in Jesus Christ.[15]

While all of these definitions are good, I would like to suggest that the definition offered by the Apostle Paul needs to be integrated with those of Fromm, Kelley, and Blood. Paul said: "This love of which I speak is slow to lose patience—it looks for a way of being constructive. It is not possessive: it is neither anxious to impress nor does it cherish inflated ideas of its own importance.

"Love has good manners and does not pursue selfish advantage. It is not touchy. It does not keep account of evil or gloat over the wickedness of other people. On the contrary, it is glad with all good men when truth prevails.

"Love knows no limit to its endurance, no end to its trust, no fading of its hope; it can outlast anything. It is, in fact, the one thing that still stands when all else has fallen."[16] This passage ought to be supplemented by the passage in Ephesians 5:21-33.

Paul's concept of love applies to all of our relationships. When we apply it to heterosexual relationships we must add to it the element of sexual love that, as Christians, we believe belongs within marriage.

### Mature Love Is a Goal

Mature love is something that we never fully achieve in this life, but rather it is a goal toward which we strive. Paul would not have held up the ideal if Christians at the churches in Corinth and Ephesus were practicing it. This is a fact that must not be overlooked. Many single young people and married couples become discouraged because they have not found perfection in their fiancé or spouse. As Christians we accept the fact that all of us are both finite and sinful. We not only make mistakes due to ignorance and poor judgment, but we also sin against one another. We say and do things that hurt.

The Christian's sanctification (the process whereby we gradually overcome sinful, selfish ways and become more like Christ) is a lifetime process. While it is true that some of us do all we can to impede the process, nonetheless, at best our sanctification is a slow, upward climb. Even though we have committed our lives to Christ, we will still disappoint and offend one another, resulting in marital conflict. Conflict is not only inevitable, but it is a sign that both spouses are thinking, growing individuals. Since there inevitably will be strain and stress, *agape* love is essential to a harmonious, successful courtship and marriage. As realists we accept the fact that there will be times when communications will break down. There will be times when we will have to repent, ask forgiveness, and seek reconciliation. But since mature love is empathic, we will be patient as we seek to understand and learn to know one another. We remember God's grace and mercy so freely given to us in Christ and we, therefore, seek to extend it to one another.

### Mature Love Has Staying Power

Because mature love is patterned after God's love which is always extended to us, we believe that mature love within marriage must be a lifetime commitment. As C. S. Lewis says, we sign a contract when we marry because we realize that there will be periods of conflict, boredom, and monotony.[17] Therefore, we pledge our word to one another saying: "I take you for better *or* for worse, for richer *or* for poorer, in sickness *as* in health, *till death do us part.*" In other words, we are saying to our spouse: "You can depend on me to stick by you—I won't walk out on you when the going gets rough!"

The modern concept of love that is promulgated by so-called humanists does not include this long-range commitment. Many non-Christians believe that love does not require the kind of commitment Christians see as essential. For them, when either partner feels that the love is gone, then there is no obligation to continue the marriage relationship. Such love is not mature love, but pure selfishness. Having said all this, I realize that there are relationships where divorce seems to be the only recourse.

Some argue that "true" love does not require a contract. They insist that when you "have to love," it is not true love at all, but duty. This kind of reasoning is specious. Since mate selection in our society is open and free (we select our own marriage partners; they are not chosen for us by our parents or a matchmaker) it makes no sense at all to say that signing a contract is compelling one to love. Actually, the traditional ritual employed by most clergymen in the wedding service exemplifies and symbolizes true or mature love. It does this when both parties freely vow that they will not permit the changing moods and seasons to affect their basic commitment to each other. Mature love has staying power.

By way of summary, then, we have said that love means many things to many people. Infatuation and romantic love are only pseudo-loves upon which a solid marriage cannot be built. While we would keep an element of romance in courtship and marriage, the only solid foundation for marriage is love that includes a preponderance of *agape* love, with *philia, storge,* and *eros* mixed in. *Agape is* needed because we are realistic about human nature and realize that courtship and marriage is a relationship in which we continue to grow. But even mature love that includes *agape* as the chief element is not a sufficient reason for marriage. As Christians we are expected to love all mankind, this includes members of the opposite sex. Rational Christian courtship and mate selection must be based upon *liking*, upon personal compatibility, and upon socioeconomic factors, as well as upon love. We will deal with these extensively in a later chapter. Let us now turn to the subject of premarital sexual ethics.

# 7

## Sex Is Not Enough

*Changing Sexual Attitudes and Practices*

Before we can discuss the issue of premarital sex it is essential that we place it in biblical and sociological perspective. Unfortunately sex is too often discussed in isolation, as if it were unrelated to the rest of life. It ought not to be treated this way. Sex must be related to the totality of life's experiences—family, church, and community, as well as to one's boy or girl friend. Furthermore, we need to begin to think of ourselves as sexual beings, and of our sexual expression as a manifestation of the kind of persons we are. Our behavior toward others really reveals not only who we think they are, but also who we think we are.

As Christians we affirm the goodness of God's creation, and this includes His creation of us as sexual beings.

Man and woman were created by Him to complement each other, to interact with each other for the enrichment of life in community. When we think of the physical demonstration of affection—necking, petting, and sexual intercourse—we believe that this, too, is good within the bonds of marriage. The physical demonstration of affection, including sexual intercourse, becomes evil only when we use it to exploit another person for our own satisfaction.

Let us return to the concept of culture as it relates to the expression of affection prior to marriage. It is too easy for us to be culture and time bound—to think that necking and petting as expressed in our society is the way it has always been, and that this is the way it is in all societies. Actually this is not the case. From antiquity to the turn of the present century, for the most part, sexual expression prior to marriage carried severe penalties. If it was practiced, as indeed it was among a minority, it was usually among the very affluent or among those who were at the other end of the social ladder. Furthermore, young people did not "date" as we know it today. Dating is really a post World War I invention. Prior to the war, one courted with a purpose—marriage. Dating just for "fun," with no particular goal in mind, is a relatively recent phenomenon which has spread to the rest of the world along with Western industrialism.

We should note also that each country has different norms or standards for male-female interaction. Anthropologists tell us that many societies permit premarital sex. Margaret Mead's writings have informed two generations about the sexual practices of those in New Guinea and Samoa.[1] While we as Christians recognize the right of each society to establish its own norms for sexual behavior, we believe that for the Christian—regardless of his society or culture—there is only one standard for premarital sexual behavior, namely, abstinence. It is interesting to note in passing, however, that every society regulates sexual behavior. The family is too basic an institution to go unregulated.

But even in the West, and in the United States in particular, we have passed through phenomenal changes in attitudes and behavior patterns with regard to premarital sex and the demonstration of affection. During the colonial period those who were found guilty of engaging in premarital sex were flogged and compelled to make public confession before the church congregation. Adulterers were compelled to wear a letter "A" or they were branded with an "A" on their forehead. While *bundling* was practiced by some, the individuals were fully clothed, wrapped in separate blankets, often with a board between them. Furthermore, they slept in the same room with the rest of the family. Courtship was brief, with betrothal and marriage following shortly thereafter. Virginity was highly prized, and woe to the young lady who brought discredit to herself and her family by becoming pregnant before marriage.[2]

Gradually, however, courtship and sexual attitudes changed from the strict puritanical standards of the colonial period to the more permissive ones of the nineteenth century. The real changes, however, did not come until the twentieth century. Courtship customs became much more liberalized, as did sex mores. As Kephart said: "The emancipation of women, accelerated urbanization, decline in secular and religious controls, a

*Sex Is Not Enough*/77

more permissive attitude on the part of the public—all tended to reduce the backlash of the Puritan tradition."[3] He cites three things that further contributed to change: (1) the automobile, (2) the availability and the mass production of contraceptives, and (3) the relatively quick and easy cure for venereal disease.[4] Most of these changes were felt after the Second World War.

The twenties brought another shift toward greater permissiveness. Women had achieved great gains legally, politically, economically, educationally, and socially. The *double standard* of sexual morality was being challenged as women demanded the same sexual freedoms men enjoyed. Dating without chaperons was now in vogue, a custom which we take for granted today. With the continued emancipation of women in the past decade, permissiveness, by contrast, seems to have gone to seed. Whereas seventy-five years ago courtship took place under the watchful eye of parents, today within ten minutes a young couple can speed away in their car unchaperoned to some quiet, secluded spot.

The point that I am making here is that dating and courtship customs *do* change. Therefore, it is the Christian's responsibility to critically evaluate these changes in the light of Christian principles. It is Christ over culture, not culture over Christ. When we turn to the Scriptures we find a definite theology of human sexuality. First of all our Lord states that "love for God and love for neighbor" are to be our guiding principles. He said in the Sermon on the Mount that adultery is a sin. He did not dwell upon premarital sex because this was not a serious problem among the youth of His day. Marriages were arranged by parents. The Apostle Paul admonishes

Christians to avoid fornication. Furthermore, he tells us that our bodies, which are the dwelling place of God's Spirit, belong to Christ, and we are not to engage them in immorality.[5]

When the Christian, therefore, thinks of physically demonstrating affection before marriage, he thinks of his obligation to God, as well as to his near neighbor—the member of the opposite sex he or she is with. Since someone he "loves" is a "neighbor," he will strive to love that person as he loves himself. Just as he would not want to be used or exploited for sexual purposes, so he does not exploit his neighbor.

### Attitudes Toward Sex Are Learned Early

Let us now turn to the subject of the acquisition of our sexual attitudes and morals. As noted earlier, we are largely the products of our family socialization. Our parents' behavior toward each other says to us, "We love each other," or "our love has grown cold." If concern and consideration for members of the family are shown by the many little things done for one another, then the children absorb the loving attitude and become loving persons too. If our parents are demonstrative in their affection, embracing and kissing in our presence, this says to us, "Affection is normal and good." Our attitude toward sex, therefore, develops early.

Later on, as we move out into our peer groups, we begin to learn the "facts of life" from a different perspective. Hopefully, if our parents have talked with us, and we have been given suitable sex education literature, we are not disturbed by the often incorrect and coarse instruction our peers give us.

### *What about Masturbation?*

During this early adolescent period we begin to become aware of the secondary sexual changes that take place during puberty. How we handle these changes depends to a large extent on our education prior to these changes. I will not go into the physiological aspects of sexual development. This has been done elsewhere and the student is referred to the bibliography for suggested readings.[6] However, I would like to say a word about masturbation. Masturbation is something that virtually all boys, and a growing number of girls, experience during adolescence. As a physician said on one occasion: "Ninety-five percent of the boys admit to masturbation and the other five percent lie about it!"

When I was a teenager I remember reading some religious tracts which said that people who masturbate go insane. Thank God we have largely passed from that benighted period. Masturbation will not drive one insane, nor will it cause warts to grow on the palm of one's hand, nor will it cause one's penis or clitoris to grow larger or waste away. I do not mean to treat the subject lightly, however, as it is not a practice to be encouraged. R. A. Sarno, in his excellent book, *Achieving Sexual Maturity*, differentiates between "habitual masturbation" and "accidental masturbation."[7] While habitual masturbation will not injure the body, it is probably a sign of some psychological problem for which the individual should seek counseling. Accidental masturbation occurs through the process of self-discovery and then is abandoned. Arno rightly points out that "solitary sex" may make it difficult for an individual to share the act of love in the mutuality of marriage, since he or she is apt to

## 80/Love and Sex Are Not Enough

bring this self-centered approach into marriage. I personally believe that one of the reasons we feel guilty about the practice is not only because we believe society frowns upon it, but because we ourselves realize that sexual satisfaction was never intended to be a solitary experience.

### Biological and Cultural Conditioning

Before we consider philosophies of premarital sex, and the pros and cons of it, let me make two important points: (1) Christians are not biologically different from non-Christians and (2) men and women differ in their expression of physical affection and in their attitudes toward sex.

While it may sound trite, it is important to make the point that being Christian does not change one's biological makeup. Our response to sexual stimuli will be the same as that of non-Christians.

Let us consider some aspects of male and female sexuality of which we should all be aware. The sex organs of women, for example, are not localized as they are in the male. They are distributed throughout the female body, e.g. her breasts are exposed, while her vagina and ovaries are inside her body. The male's genitals, however, while localized in the groin, are outside of the body cavity. Also, while men experience a buildup of seminal fluid, women do not—a fact which many believe is significant. As one gynecologist punned: "That makes a *vas deferens*!" Not only is man designed biologically to be the aggressor, but our culture encourages him to be aggressive, whereas women are designed biologically to be receptive and they are nurtured to be passive.

Therefore, both for biological and cultural reasons men are generally recognized as being erotic, whereas women are seen as romantic.

Christian young men become just as easily aroused sexually by visual stimuli (pictures, literature, persons) and by physical contact with members of the opposite sex as non-Christians. Christian young women, also, respond to physical contact, and to expressions of affection, just as non-Christian girls do. The point that I am making is simply that Christians are biologically no different from others when it comes to sexuality.

It is important to realize, also, that beyond a certain point of physical intimacy, biology overtakes reason! Christians can get "carried away" and lose control just as easily as anyone else. Witness the number of "hurry up marriages" in your church, community, or on your campus. Therefore, it is important for Christian young people to think through their philosophy of sexual expression realistically and to make sure reason prevails in these matters.

Second, we should be aware of the fundamental differences in attitude and temperament between men and women. These differences are due both to our biological makeup and to the impact of our culture upon us. It might be helpful to list some of the important differences.

| Men | Women |
|---|---|
| Biologically built to be aggressive | Anatomically built to be receptive |
| Erotic | Romantic |

| | |
|---|---|
| Tendency to separate sex and love | Tendency to correlate sex with love |
| Culturally conditioned to be exploitive | Culturally conditioned to be trusting and sharing |
| Subconsciously think, "If she's a 'good' girl she'll not have sex." | Tendency to think, "Since we're in love and he wants to have sex, I'll yield." |

While there are exceptions to the generalizations made above, for the most part Christians have been socialized by their peers and the mass media to respond in somewhat the same manner as non-Christians. On the one hand, if a woman loves a man, she tends to be trusting and may yield to his affectionate advances. The male, on the other hand, if he is serious about a girl, hopes that she will not be easy to engage—even as he makes advances. Because of these differences, young people would find it helpful to write out their philosophy of sex or affectional expression. Discussing these views with their boy or girl friend may help them come to some consensus about their sexual relationships and help both maintain their Christian principles.

### Four Premarital Sex Standards

At this point let me share four premarital sexual standards which Ira L. Reiss has identified.[8] The first is the *single standard* which we identify as conservative and Christian. This standard insists that both men and women should abstain from sexual intercourse before marriage. While the contemporary sexual revolution has taken its toll on this, it still remains the ideal for Christians.

The *double standard* is a second one. This standard is popular in both the Eastern and Western world. It has always been challenged by Christians, and more recently by the women's liberation movement. The biblical commandment to abstain from fornication applies equally to both men and women. With regard to the liberation movement, women are saying that if men can engage in premarital sex, then so can they. Recent statistics indicate an increase in the number of women engaging in premarital sex. This has caused some men to reconsider the validity of the double standard.

The third standard is *permissiveness with affection,* the idea that it's all right to engage in premarital sex if you're "in love." This notion is quite popular in our society, especially among college students. Class surveys I have taken over the past few years indicate that most of my students prefer this standard. One of the difficulties with this standard is that one does not know how long the affection will last. Since over 50 percent of engagements are believed to be broken, it should cause young people to think carefully about the time and place of sexual intercourse. If it is the expression of love one hopes to share with a wife or husband, wouldn't it be best to wait until one is actually married?

*Permissiveness without affection* is the fourth standard of premarital sex. This philosophy says that sexual intercourse is no different from eating—it is a bodily function that gives pleasure and, therefore, premarital sex is a normal experience and should cause no guilt. While individuals who subscribe to this view are often brash and vocal, it is quite possible that their bravado and braggadocio are attempts to cover up a deep-seated sense of insecurity and feeling of personal inadequacy. One psychologist reports that "bed-hopping" is often a sign of neurosis.[9] It is, after all, difficult to satisfy an inner psychological or spiritual need for love and security by a physical act devoid of genuine caring. Robert Blood's observations, after discussing these standards, are worth noting. "Before I became a sociologist, I was against sexual conservatism," he says. "However, the longer I have studied the evidence from scientific research, the more I have been forced to recognize the positive consequences of restraint. . . . Waiting [until marriage to have sexual intercourse] has two long-range advantages: (1) it provides a secure setting for children conceived from sexual intercourse; (2) drawing a sexual distinction between 'not married' and marriage accentuates the importance of marriage and contributes to its stability."[10]

## Rationalizations for Premarital Sex

With all the talk about sex in schools and colleges today, as well as in the mass media, it is inevitable that Christian young people will be challenged to defend their standard of sexual morality. Therefore, it might be well to state the pros and cons of premarital sex. I am drawing upon the rationalizations for premarital sex that Kephart mentions in his marriage text, with modifications.[11]

The first is the *physiological release* argument. This is used by men who argue that there is a biological buildup of seminal fluid which needs to be released. Therefore, if the girl really loves him, so the argument goes, she will consent to sexual intercourse. The obvious response to this argument is that there is no medical evidence that sexual restraint results in psychological or physiological harm. In fact, nature provides for release through nocturnal emissions or "wet dreams." Also, masturbation is a common practice which provides release.

Another argument is the *"other society"* one. This is one used by students who have read about other cultures with mores that differ from our own. Many nonliterate societies permit premarital sex. Therefore, the argument goes, since it is done in "New Guinea," why not here in the United States? The response notes that cultural traits usually form a consistent pattern—they support one another. We cannot lift practices and transfer them unless we are willing to integrate them fully into our culture. Besides, from a Christian perspective we would argue that these are non-Christian cultures and not relevant to our situation. What others do is never justification for what *we* do.

The *bandwagon* argument is the third. In this we are told that everyone is doing it. Therefore, we should get on the bandwagon. Actually everyone is not doing it! While the incidence of premarital sex has increased, it is by no means the universal practice. Sexual statistics are difficult to acquire, and the trustworthiness of the information is suspect. Furthermore, many of those who have engaged in premarital sex report that they did so with their fiancé, or on one or two occasions. In any case, as Christians we do not base our ethical standards on statistics, but on Christian principles. No one would argue that since most Americans drink, and many drive while under the influence of alcohol, that everyone should be permitted to drive while intoxicated.

The fourth argument is the *hedonistic* or pleasure argument which states that sexual intercourse is a pleasurable experience. Why, therefore, shouldn't we enjoy it? After all, if two consenting adults agree, and no one is hurt by it, why should society object? The question is: "What are the criteria of measurement?" Are we talking about the short-run or the long-run? While there may not *appear* to be any immediate negative consequences, there may well be long-range ones. For one thing, it is worth noticing that many parents who were once permissive now have switched in their thinking to the conservative single standard.[12] Apparently the short-range pleasure did not outweigh the long-range pain they experienced. While a couple may reap some pleasure from premarital sex, unintended consequences such as (1) pregnancy, (2) venereal disease, (3) guilt, (4) dissolution of the relationship, (5) loss of self-respect, and (6) early marriage due to pregnancy, may turn the joy to mourning. For the Christian the hedonistic argument is invalid because one is not free to derive pleasure by willfully violating a clear-cut Christian prohibition.

A fifth argument is that "*If you really love me* you'll have intercourse with me and prove it." This argument is one of the most frequently used. Of course, the perfect squelch is, "If you really love me, why do you ask me to violate my ethical standards?" It is wise to keep in mind that love can be a fragile emotion. The Old Testament tells of Amnon's affair with Tamar. It is interesting to note the comment of the writer regarding Amnon's feelings after intercourse with Tamar. "Then Amnon hated her [Tamar] with very great hatred; so that the hatred

*Sex Is Not Enough*/87

with which he hated her was greater than the love with which he had loved her."[13] Jeremiah tells us that "the heart is deceitful above all things, and desperately corrupt; who can understand it?"[14] It is difficult to second-guess the response after an experience of sexual intimacy outside of marriage—even with someone we "love."

Finally, there is the *compatibility* argument. This one raises the question, "How can we be sure we are compatible sexually unless we try it?" This argument is not valid for several reasons. Kephart presents a couple of hypothetical cases. Couple "A" is compatible in every way, except sexually. They find that when they test for sexual compatibility, they experience some difficulty. Should they break off their engagement? And what if couple "B" are compatible sexually, but ill suited in most other areas? Should they marry on the basis of their physical compatibility? David Ruben, in an article in *Redbook*, observed that premarital sexual compatibility in no way guarantees sexual compatibility in marriage, since we cannot simulate the actual married experience. When one is married he assumes an entirely new set of roles and responsibilities which make married sex different.

Furthermore, as Kephart implies, there is a great deal more to compatibility within marriage than the sexual aspect, as important as I believe that is. God has made us so that virtually any two people can relate physically. The female vagina is elastic and flexible; it can accommodate the male penis, whether small or large, without any difficulty. "Plumbing," or the physical fit, is not the determining factor in sexual compatibility, and neither is technique. Sexual intercourse is basically a spiritual experience. If two people are communicating and are attuned to one another, then, and only then, can true sexual compatibility be achieved.

From a Christian perspective there is no logical reason why the two states, courtship and marriage, should be confused. It is difficult for me to separate the notion of exploitation from premarital sex—it is difficult to get away from the notion that one person is using another, or both are using each other. As Christians we see sexual intercourse as a vital part of marriage, something beautiful that needs to be shared on a regular basis within marriage.[15] From a Christian perspective, sexual intercourse is the one expression of love that should be restricted until the couple is willing and ready to assume complete responsibility for the total well-being of each other.

Since I have been emphasizing the ideal Christian standard, the single standard, I do not mean to imply that if one has had premarital sex, he has committed the unpardonable sin. The grace of God that forgives us for other sins, also provides for forgiveness of sexual sins. Nonetheless, it is true that premarital sexual intercourse is a different kind of sin. Paul says that "any other sin a man commits does not affect his body; but the man who commits immorality sins against his own body."[16] Since the sex act involves more than the physical union of two persons, it is one of the most intimate of all human experiences, and it is virtually impossible to forget. However, the Bible does assure us that God's forgiveness awaits all who freely repent and turn to Him.

By way of conclusion, I would reiterate a thesis of this book. While sex is certainly an integral part of the married relationship, it is far from being the sum total of it.

Just because we love someone, and just because we have sexual desires for a person, are not sufficient reasons for marriage. There are many sociological factors that should enter into mate selection. Let us turn to a consideration of some of them now.

# 8

## Principles of Mate Selection

Success within marriage depends more on the choice of a compatible marriage partner, than on anything that occurs after one is married. For this reason marriage is not something that should be rushed into. There is a direct correlation between length of courtship, the age at marriage, and the stability of the marriage. The longer the courtship and the older one is (mid-twenties), the better. If we are dispassionate and rational, if we take time really to get to know our prospective partner, then we will know whether or not he or she would make a good marriage partner. If we find that there are too many basic differences in temperament, values, beliefs, role definitions, and aspirations, then the relationship should be severed. If there was no serious physical involvement in the relationship, then the couple will experience less psychological trauma. It can be regarded as a learning experience which should make us wiser in future relationships.

In courtship it is not love alone that enables a couple to succeed, nor is it sexual involvement that enhances the relationship. But it is the sociological factors that really provide the basis for a mature loving relationship in marriage. Before we discuss some of the factors that are relevant to a successful marriage, let me emphasize that a perfect match is not possible. Just as most young men have constructed an ideal type of mate who probably does not exist, so have young women. The chances of finding someone who measures up to our ideal is quite remote. While it is good to construct an ideal type, it is well to realize that you will have to modify it when you eventually meet him or her. In fact the ability to change and adapt is a significant factor in marital adjustment, as well as during courtship.

We should not, however, select a mate with the idea of changing him or her. Marriage counselors virtually all agree that it is one thing for you to change yourself, but it is quite another thing for you to change your spouse. If you want to fail at marriage, marry with that goal in mind. Face reality; if you are not compatible before marriage, you will be even less compatible afterward. Moses, Paul, and Jesus said that when two marry they should become one. This does not mean, as the O'Neills caricature in their controversial book, *Open Marriage*, that each partner in marriage must lose his individual identity.[1] It does mean, however, that we must agree on basics, otherwise there cannot be the unity, peace, and communication necessary within marriage and the family.

### Endogamous Factors

Let us now look at some of the endogamous or social factors generally regarded as being relevant to a good match. Race, religion, ethnicity, and socioeconomic class status are regarded as the interlocking endogamous factors.

*Race.* The question naturally arises, "Should I be open to marrying someone of another race?" From a Christian and a moral point of view there is no reason why you may not marry someone of another race or ethnic group.[2] While it is not immoral, it requires two individuals who are both compatible and determined that they will make the marriage work.

All sorts of questions, however, need to be raised. If we are speaking about longstanding fellow citizens of another race, this is one thing; but if we are speaking about recent immigrants or temporary residents who belong to another culture, this is quite another. What may appear as exotic, mysterious, and exciting for a while, will become monotonous, common place, and humdrum in time, especially if you left North America to live abroad. If you do plan to marry someone from another country, it would be wise to go and live in his or her community for a few months to see what it will be like.

One should ask questions such as : "Is the person of the same religion, and of the same socioeconomic class?" "Do we share a common educational and intellectual level?" "Are our values basically the same?" These are crucial factors.

The fact that the divorce rate is higher among those who marry outside of their race should not be overlooked. Many sociologists believe that we live in a racist society. This is probably true, but what is true of the United States and Canada is equally or more true of other nations. Therefore, the question of race needs to be carefully considered.

If the couple are compatible in religion, socioeconomic class status, lifestyle, and the like, there is no reason why the couple could not make a go of the marriage if they work at it. A racially mixed marriage, however, does require greater effort. The couple must be willing to face the problems that will inevitably arise because of the prejudice and discriminatory practices that exist in our society. While it is not immoral to marry outside one's race, it probably is unwise.

*Religion.* Most couples marry within their own faith—Protestants marry Protestants, Roman Catholics marry Roman Catholics, Jews marry Jews, and the nonreligious and nominally religious marry those with a similar outlook. They marry within their own faith because religion really symbolizes a subculture within our pluralistic society.[3] Andrew W. Greeley, in his book *The Denominational Society,* maintains that denominations serve as quasi-ethnic groups with which we form a positive identity. Young people are socialized into one of these denominational subcultures within our society. Individuals who marry within their own denominational subculture have a lower divorce rate than those who marry outside it.[4] One reason why the divorce rate is lower in such cases is that you can take more for granted. Not only can you worship and serve God from a sense of oneness, but you can do so without having to stop to explain, justify, and defend your faith and subcultural traits. Furthermore, when conflict arises, if the religions are different, they often become the focus for further conflict. But not only is it important that a Christian marry a Christian—one's denominational affiliation is also important. Even within denominations there is often a wide range of perspectives, from the extreme conservative and fundamentalist to the moderate and liberal. It is not wise for a fundamentalist Baptist who does not smoke, drink, or dance to marry a "liberal" American Baptist or Lutheran who sees nothing wrong with those things, and many other practices besides.

Religion becomes an integral part of our lives; we internalize beliefs—they become second nature. As a pastor and counselor I have met scores of couples who before marriage said that religion was not important, only to find themselves rebelling at having to baptize or not baptize their child and, also, refusing to identify with their spouse's faith because they feel "they just can't!" If your Christian faith means anything to you, then it would be wise to not only avoid dating those of other faiths, but also to wait until you meet someone with whom you can grow in grace and knowledge, and in service to Christ.

*Ethnicity.* By ethnicity we mean those who identify with a specific nationality and its subculture. Glazer and Moynihan and Novack have shown that the various immigrant groups that settled in the United States have not "melted down" into one homogeneous culture.[5] Furthermore, Americans and Canadians are presently committed to pluralism in our nation, and we are supporting the efforts of ethnics to retain their cultural heritage. Of course, the ethnic commitment of the first-generation immigrant is generally much stronger than that of subsequent generations. Also, within ethnic groups the socioeconomic class is a significant variable. We would probably find that upper-class and middle-class Jewish, Irish, and Polish individuals have more in common than two persons of a single nationality from opposite ends of the continuum—upper and lower.

Ethnic background does not constitute the barrier it once did, however, especially in communities where a given ethnic group is small in number, and in those where relationships are harmonious. For example, B. R. Bugelski found that the rate of intermarriage between Italian and Polish increased steadily between 1930 and 1960.[6] Although concern over ethnicity has diminished, there still seems to be concern about marrying within one's faith. Italians and Polish people are largely Roman Catholic. Will Herberg sees the United States becoming a nation in which one's religion—Protestantism, Catholicism, Judaism—is more important than ethnic background.[7] The question, therefore, is: How committed is each individual to his ethnic subculture? Conceivably, a first-generation Russian-American would find it rather difficult relating to a third-generation American of Russian extraction.

*Socioeconomic Class.* Many of us would like to believe that we live in a classless society. While it is true that North Americans are not highly class conscious, we nonetheless do have the broad strata of upper, middle, working, and lower classes. These are not distinct categories but continuous ones—they blend into one another and overlap considerably. Depending upon the age and size of our community, these strata could probably each be divided into at least two parts—an upper and a lower category within each class.

People usually fall into one of the classes on the basis of education, occupation, and income. Each class, generally speaking, has a style of life which members take for granted. We do not think about our class identity; for the most part we merely act it out. We find ourselves almost instinctively being attracted or repelled by the behavior of individuals and groups within other classes of society because "we just don't do things that way!" Often we become quite conscious of class differences when we visit in the home of someone from another stratum—we sense the differences not only because of the contrast in neighborhood, decor, esthetic taste, and amenities, but also in the behavior of those within the home.

Since membership in a given socioeconomic class means that we have adopted the values, beliefs, and practices of that subculture, it is important that we do not dip too far down or reach up too high when we think about choosing a marriage partner. Sociologists observe that men tend to marry within their own class or down, while women generally marry within their own class or up. With a little bit of thought and imagination one can think of innumerable problems that can arise if the gap is too wide. Tastes in music, art, literature, entertainment, recreation, dress, and food, as well as differences in the use of language and religious expression, all reflect our socioeconomic status. If a fellow marries a girl too far above him, can he keep her in the manner to which she has become accustomed? If a girl marries down, can she live comfortably with her husband if he has a different lifestyle and set of values? And what about compatibility with his family? Unfortunately, when young people are "in love," they fail to consider the practicalities of everyday life. If differences are too great, this means there are bound to be significant differences in subcultures and lifestyles which could prove insurmountable. Nonetheless, if there is a basic commitment to similar values—with great effort, with a long and realistic courtship, and with much give and a little take on the part of each—the marriage could work.

Now these four variables are all interrelated. Those of similar religious faith and nationality tend to live in the same neighborhood. Those of the same socioeconomic class tend to attend the same or similar type denominations. Obviously if the difference in one of these areas is slight, it is not significant; but if the difference in one or more is great, it is a matter worth serious consideration.

### Homogamous Factors

In addition to the endogamous factors mentioned above, some attention should be given to homogamous factors (similarity of psychological, physical, and personal attributes). One homogamous factor is usually that of *age*. Most couples are relatively close in age. The average difference between men and women at marriage is about three years, with the male being the older. While some have advocated that men marry women older than themselves because the life expectancy of women is greater than that of men, this has not found much favor with either sex.

Age differences, of course, are more significant if the spread is four, five, or more years when one partner is very young. Five years difference when one is fifteen is more significant than when the youngest is twenty or twenty-five. The questions that come to mind are: "Why is a person that old choosing to date someone so young?" "Why is a person that young choosing to date someone so old?" "Is he or she too immature?" "Is he or she looking for a mother or father image and/or surrogate?" "Can he or she not relate to someone his own age?" Also, there is concern over what difference the age span will make in socializing with each other's friends, or later on in life.

In addition to age, some consideration should be given to homogamy of personal habits. Differences in important personal habits and interests (such as the use of alcohol and tobacco) could cause serious problems. For someone who was reared in a family and church subculture that regarded the use of alcohol as sinful, the use of it by a fiancé or spouse could be quite disturbing. Some young people have had unfortunate experiences with alcoholism in their homes and they shudder at the prospects of coping with it in their own marriage. In such cases it would be best to break off a relationship, especially when one feels very strongly about the use of alcohol. It is difficult to change habits that are well established, unless one decides for himself that it is injurious to his health and/or morally wrong.

Sometimes an individual will issue an ultimatum, "Either give up alcohol and smoking or the relationship is off!" What often happens in a case like this is that the "offending person" will stop until after marriage, and then revert to his or her old habits. It is best to sever a relationship when an impasse has been reached over something that one party regards as crucial, rather than continuing ostrich like, pretending that it does not exist or hoping that it will go away. Remember, it is the choice of a compatible mate *before* marriage, more than anything that one does *after* marriage, that will determine one's happiness *in* marriage.

What we have said about habits such as the use of alcohol and tobacco apply even more so to personality factors such as a *hot temper, jealousy, the use of sarcasm and profane language, moodiness, cynicism,* and the like. We do not change in character and personality merely because we go through the ritual of a marriage ceremony. Courtship is regarded by many as an artificial and, often, abnormal relationship since both parties are putting their "best foot forward." Objectionable personality and character traits usually become more pronounced after marriage when we "become ourselves." Therefore, the courtship should be long enough and realistic enough to enable one to learn to know the other person's vices as well as his virtues.

Blood suggests that similarity of temperament is another important factor to consider. He says, "By temperament I mean the physiological activity level and response pattern of the individual."[8] Some individuals are a "ball of fire" all day, while others do not wake up until they've had their second cup of coffee. Some are night people, while others are ready for bed at 9:00 or 10:00 p.m. While such variables are not sufficient reasons for discontinuing a relationship, too many such differences could create serious conflict.

In addition to homogamy of temperament, Blood suggests other areas in which needs should be parallel or similar. If the husband is *achievement oriented*, then it would be best if he chose a young lady for a wife who is also achievement oriented—one who will either support him in his career aspirations or join in pursuing a career of her own. Often I have met men in the ministry whose wives did not share their sense of "call." Their lack of support was a definite hindrance in the performance of their husbands' ministerial role. I believe that the concept of parallel needs that Blood introduces is significant because an individual's career can yield a great deal of satisfaction in life.

Likewise, some men or women are *affiliational*—they feel the need to be close to other people. They like to be home-based. They want to center their life around their spouse, children, kin, and friends. In this case it would be disastrous if they married a person who had to move several times during his career, or a social extrovert who wanted to be on the go continually.

In addition to the above personal traits, sociological research supports the idea that we marry people who are generally as physically attractive and as intelligent as we are, as well as someone with similar social attitudes.

Men seem to put greater stock in physical appearance than women. They notice the face and the figure. While women are aware of the physique and the looks of the male, they seem to be more concerned with the total personality. Since physical beauty is only skin deep, both sexes would be wise to give greater attention to character traits—the total personality.

There are other roles in marriage besides the sex role, and it is important that these be considered before marriage. Vernard Eller, in his book *A Sex Manual for Pu-*

*ritans*, rightly points out that when geologists search for oil, they do not look for oil on the surface of the ground, but in certain rock formations.[9] The male, therefore, would do well to probe beyond the physique for the kind of character formation that produces a personality that will stand the test of time—one that does not need to be supported with "aids" marketed by Madison Avenue.

Education and intelligence are two other homogamous factors that contribute to a couple's compatibility. I do not mean to equate formal schooling with intelligence. The two are not necessarily synonymous! But having said that, it is important that a couple be compatible intellectually. John Milton went so far as to suggest that the inability "to communicate" constituted grounds for divorce.[10] While I do not concur in this, I see intellectual compatibility as being very important. I believe that marriage ought to be deferred until both are well on their way to achieving their basic educational goals. Intellectually, girls who drop out of college to put their husbands through school tend to arrest their own intellectual development—unless they make a special effort to remain alert. Furthermore, all too often the male comes to feel he has "outgrown" the wife who sacrificed her own career to put him through college and/or graduate school.

With regard to social attributes (religious, economic, political, and social views), the evidence supports the belief that individuals with similar views are those who continue a dating relationship into courtship and marriage. This does not mean that couples are in perfect agreement on everything; no two people ever are. Nor would this be desirable. There would be no growth! Unless there is basic agreement, however, the relationship would be strained, at best.

## Theories of Mate Selection

In addition to the endogamous and homogamous factors we have just examined, it would be helpful to review several theories of mate selection which should shed some light on the courtship process.[11] No one theory offers foolproof guidance, but considered together they can be quite helpful.

One theory that is psychoanalytical in origin states that an individual selects as a partner one whose personality and physical appearance resembles that of his opposite sex parent. Men are believed to be more influenced by the *parental image* than women. While there is no conclusive evidence to support the parental image theory, those who identify favorably with their parents may unconsciously be influenced in this way. It is worth noting, however, that by the time young people are old enough to date seriously, their parents have had about twenty to twenty-five years to work at resolving conflicts and developing a harmonious relationship. It is unreasonable to assume, therefore, that one could find someone like Mom or Dad.

The *role theory* suggests that an individual will marry someone who shares similar sex role concepts. The young lady, for example, who believes that the male should be the head of the home and exercise a leadership role, is not likely to choose a "Casper Milquetoast" or a submissive male as a marriage partner. It is only common sense that basic agreement on wife-husband, mother-father roles would contribute to a more harmonious marriage than one in which there is constant conflict over basics. John Scanzoni treats this subject effectively in his book, *Sexual Bargaining*.[12] Most difficulties arise in marriage because of basic differences which generate secondary conflict. A profitable exercise for couples contemplating marriage would be to write an analysis of the roles played by their parents, discussing their own concepts in the light of them, and deciding how they would change them, if at all.

A third theory holds that an individual often selects a marriage partner who shares similar *values*. R. H. Coombs believes that the social factors we discussed earlier provide the ground out of which our values grow. This theory probably operates more than we realize since, like birds, we tend to "flock" with those who share the same values and interests that we do. If a couple like the same things, generally speaking, they will not only enjoy each other's company, but they will also enjoy their leisure time activities together. One of the tragedies of a mixed religion marriage is that both individuals often end up giving up their faith and withdrawing from the fellowship of their church.[13]

A fourth theory is that of *complementary needs*. R. F. Winch advanced this theory which states that we select as partners those who will complement our needs. Therefore, if a male feels the need to be dominant, he should select a female who believes she should be submissive. Similarly, if the female likes to be outwardly demonstrative in her affection, she should select someone who enjoys receiving affection. Again, if one likes to achieve, he or she should select someone who likes to give support and to achieve vicariously through his or her mate. While Winch's research confirmed his theory, subsequent research has not uniformly supported his hypothesis. This theory, however, seems to make sense. It would be wise to marry someone who complements your needs, not only in Winch's sense, but also in another sense. If one is weak in one area, it would be wise to select someone who is strong in the same area. Therefore, by choosing such a person, both would benefit.

A fifth theory I would like to present briefly is the *filter theory* of Kerckhoff and Davis. At the risk of oversimplifying, their research suggests that couples progressively filter out possible partners through a series of screening devices. At first we unconsciously use social factors to filter out those who are not from the same general socioeconomic, religious, racial, and/or ethnic group. Then, second, we eliminate those from our endogamous grouping who do not share similar values. Third, we select from the group someone with similar values, learning to know him or her more intimately, allowing need-complementarity to determine whether or not the relationship should continue. Thus, Kerckhoff and Davis are suggesting that we begin with endogamous factors, move on to values, and then to need-complementarity. It seems to me that this is the process through which courtship ought to move, and in many cases does. At any place along the way, or within the process, if we realize that the other person is not suitable, we can break off the relationship.

All these theories have some merit. When coupled with, and related to the endogamous (social) and homogamous (psychological and person) factors, they can prove helpful as we reflect upon the important task of mate selection and marriage.

## Roles Within Marriage

When we consider mate selection, it is not only helpful to consider many of the endogamous and homogamous factors, and the theories of mate selection, but it is also well to reflect upon the roles to be played within marriage. Usually the chief role we play in courtship is a recreational one, the same one we play during adolescence in our fun culture. Therefore, it comes naturally. But if we are to approach mate selection rationally, and not emotionally, we need to consider other roles that will be played within marriage in addition to the recreational one. We need to ask, on the basis of a courtship of reasonable length, whether or not he or she fills these roles to "my satisfaction." Nye and Berardo point out the changing roles of husbands and wives in our society.[14] While it is true that institutions have usurped from the family many of its functions, there still remain several crucial roles which deserve our consideration.

For the male there is the *provider role* which not only requires vocational and professional skills, but also interpersonal skills. Most positions today require lengthy periods of education. Each position carries with it a status, and *it is still largely true that it is the status of the husband that the wife inherits*. Therefore, it would be wise for the young lady not to rush into an engagement before she can see where the young man will be going vocationally. She should ask herself, "Will I be satisfied with the community status his position will provide?"

Status not only includes a given level of income, but a particular lifestyle. Despite women's lib, most wives still do identify with their husband's status which seems to carry greater weight than their own.

Another role is that of *the socialization of children*. A man might make an exciting date, but will he make a good father for your children? Does he have the strength of character, the reliability, and the unselfishness needed? Eventually, most couples want to have children. Therefore it makes sense to think ahead, projecting him into those roles. If you feel that he does not have the sense of discipline and commitment needed, does he really have the kind of qualities you desire in a husband-father? Likewise, is the effervescent female date apt to have the qualities you want in a wife-mother?

Nye and Berardo identify three other roles which they designate as emerging male roles; they are the recreational, the therapeutic, and the sexual intercourse roles. The *recreational role* was minimal in our grandparents' day. Then, it was only the prerogative of an affluent minority. Today, however, at least 80 percent of Americans enjoy the use of some discretionary money that they can use for vacationing—at least for short periods of time. If we are to enjoy leisure activities, it is important that there be some consensus between husbands and wives on how their time will be spent. Since most Americans and Canadians still subscribe to a mild form of patriarchal family structure, the husband's leadership here is important.

The second emerging male role is the *therapeutic* one. By this Nye and Berardo mean that the husband needs to be a "personal problem solver." He needs to be there when his wife needs him—to listen, to understand, and to empathize. Jessie Bernard says, "One of the major functions of positive expressive talk is to raise the status of the other, to give help, to reward; in ordinary human relations, it performs the stroking function. As infants need physical caressing or stroking in order to live and grow, even to survive, so also do adults need emotional or psychological stroking or caressing to remain normal."[15] The husband serves as a sounding board for his wife as she resolves her problems.

The third emerging male role within marriage is that of *sexual intercourse*. Prior to the sexual revolution that David R. Mace says took place in the last century, sex was something that men, not women, were supposed to enjoy. Now sexual intercourse is regarded as something to be mutually enjoyed by both wife and husband.[16] Nye and Berardo, however, suggest that in marriage the sex role for the male may be considered a *work role*, since men are obligated to see that their wives find the experience enjoyable also. Since sexual intercourse is to be an act of communion, a mutual sharing, it seems to me that it is demeaning to refer to it as a "work role." In this connection one of the negative consequences of premarital sex, especially among those who are promiscuous, is that they develop exploitive techniques which become habitual. These exploitive techniques are then carried into marriage where they prove dysfunctional. Premarital sex has a tendency to be "body centered" sex and not "person centered," and this type of sex must then be unlearned within marriage if sex relations are to become an act of mutual love.

A role that I would add, which is not an emerging role

but an old role which needs to be reasserted, is the role of the husband-father as the "spiritual leader." The Judeo-Christian faith has traditionally supported the idea that the husband and father should exercise spiritual leadership within the family. While some might immediately object, suggesting that I am denying the equality of the sexes, I do not believe this to be the case. *Equality does not mean sameness*. The Apostle Paul obviously did not mean that roles were to be interchangeable when he said: "So there is no difference between . . . men and women; you are all one in union with Christ Jesus."[17] Men and women are indeed of equal value in God's sight, but this does not mean that the roles are necessarily "up for grabs." The husband is responsible to God for the total well-being of the family. Two individuals cannot be the leader, and within the Judeo-Christian tradition the male has had this responsibility. Therefore, the woman should marry someone whom she can respect—someone whom she can look up to in this leadership role.

Just as the wife must be aware of the roles her future husband will play, so must the husband be aware of the roles his future wife will play—there must be understanding and agreement for a harmonious relationship. Let us consider some of the female roles within marriage.

In the past the wife used to play a *provider role*—she worked not only in the home, but also out in the field beside her husband. In fact, Alice Rossi insists that women have always worked extremely hard about the home, in addition to playing *the homemaker and caretaker of children roles*.[18] She says that it has only been in the past few decades that the latter roles have been the only ones for a majority of women. Therefore, what we are witnessing today—the return of the provider role to women—is really a recapturing of a role that they temporarily lost. The big difference, however, is that women are now leaving home to do the work. The male must think through this matter of the female role in society. From a Christian perspective, the Scriptures say nothing about the woman being confined to the homemaker and child socializing roles. In our day, however, with the lack of support that used to be provided by the extended family, many women have chosen to remain at home, especially while the children are under school age.

The *child care and child socialization roles* have also changed over the years. We have passed through cycles, from being restrictive to being permissive, and all shades in between. Part of the fluctuation is due to the fact that middle-class parents lack confidence in their own ability to rear children, and they have looked to "authorities" whose opinions have also vacillated. In a film on child rearing, Dr. Spock made the point that most parents are naturally equipped to rear children, and he suggested that they should use their own common sense in doing so. While he obviously did not mean that we should not consult specialists or read good literature, he suggests that we are too preoccupied with what the "authorities" have to say. He also added that no matter what we do as parents, our children will not like us 100 percent of the time. Therefore, we should discipline (instruct) them to the best of our ability.

Part of the difficulty is due to the near demise of the traditional extended family, with all of its familial supports. This has resulted in the shifting of almost the entire burden for child rearing and nurture upon parents within the nuclear family—especially the mother. To ameliorate this situation, the father must be co-opted into a more active role. This is difficult, however, since his work takes him outside of the home the major part of the day. This is often further compounded by the career-oriented wife-mother.

The wife's *housekeeper role* has drastically changed from one of producer (on the farm) to one of consumer (in the urban area). Her primary responsibility is not gardening and canning, but wise shopping. Whereas her burden has been lightened by labor saving appliances, she actually has no more time because she must do most of the chores herself. While the newlywed wife would probably find time weighing heavily upon her hands, the mother with a few children of school age probably has more than enough to do. Therefore, the wife-mother who chooses not to labor outside the home is not "just a housewife"; she has taken on a "management position."

In addition to the above roles, women also have to assume new *recreational and therapeutic roles*. Blood's and Wolfe's research among housewives indicates that wives rate companionship above "love."[19] Therefore, it is important that both spouses share common interests in order that their leisure time might be meaningfully shared. While it is true that "togetherness" has been grossly exaggerated, and that each individual will inevitably have unique interests of his own, nonetheless, a good portion of the leisure time will be spent together. Under these circumstances then, there should be some mutuality of interests or both will suffer from loneliness and/or frustration.

The therapeutic role, likewise, is just as important for the female as it is for the male. Mace suggests that while women have a tendency to speak when they are troubled, men tend to become silent.[20] He sees the role of the wife as one of "drawing the husband out," and encouraging him to air his frustrations, anxieties, and concerns. Blood suggests that one way the therapeutic role can be fulfilled is by setting aside between ten to fifteen minutes each evening for socializing, perhaps when one or both return home from work. If there are children who are old enough to understand, they should be taught that this time is for mother and dad to share together. The children will have ample time later to visit with their parents. Bowman suggests that the couple can use symbols or signs to convey to each other what kind of a day they have had. If they have had a bad day and one or the other needs a sympathetic ear, they can alert one another. For example, a wife might wear her apron backwards, or the husband might whistle or throw in his hat as he enters the house. While this may sound a bit corny, it serves two purposes: it informs your spouse that you have had a bad day, and it also reminds you that you are irritated, making you more sensitive to what you might say to your spouse.

### *Marriage and Career Patterns*

Another aspect of roles in marriage relates to the wife's work inside and outside the home. Nye and Berardo have adapted Clifford Kirkpatrick's delineation of the "homemaker" and "career" roles within marriage.[21] Let us turn our attention to the choices which are open to a woman, since her choice will have an important effect upon marital interaction. The first option is the *maternity-homemaking pattern* in which the wife is not gainfully employed outside the home. In this traditional pattern she is a nurturer of children, homemaker, and involved in volunteer activities such as church, PTA, garden club, and the like. Many couples may start out with a traditional pattern, but later switch to another as their views change and/or their children mature.

The second is the *companion pattern.* In this "the wife eliminates or minimizes maternal and economic productivity roles. Rather, it might be said that she stresses sexual, recreational, and therapeutic ones, devoting her time to personal attractiveness and centering her life about the interests and activities of her husband." In other words, she is husband-centered rather than child-centered or career-centered. She seeks to be a companion in all areas, emphasizing the therapeutic, recreational, and sexual roles. It seems to me that this one makes good sense in the light of the family life-cycle. Since the average couple spend more years together without children than with children, it only makes sense for the husband and wife to put each other first. Many times when married couples have domestic difficulties they lose themselves in their children, only to face the fact that when the children are gone, they have nothing in common and cannot communicate with one another. Legally they live together, but spiritually and psychologically they have grown steadily apart.

The *career pattern* is the third option. In this pattern the wife pursues her career and maintains it throughout the marriage. Any children the couple has are planned for so as not to interfere with her career. (I heard of one woman teacher who had six children, all born during the summer so that she would not have to give up her teaching career! That's real family planning!) At home, work will be shared equally, being supplemented by the various service businesses.

Still a fourth alternative is the *family-plus-partial-career* pattern. Many women follow this pattern which enables them to give their primary attention to their children and husband, and a portion of their time to some public work—a position outside the home. Wives often work until the first child comes, then drop out of the work force, reentering partially when the last child begins school. Eventually they may or may not fully enter the work force when the children are through college or "out of the nest."

Which familial structure the wife and husband select is a matter of personal preference. Individuals will vary in their judgment. The important thing is that the couple reach some consensus before they marry on which pattern is best for them.

### Authority Patterns Within Marriage

Related to roles is the question of where the authority will lie within the family. *Traditionally the authority has been vested in the male.* Biblically speaking, the male is to be "head of the home," with his wife and children looking to him for leadership. Gibson Winter believes that the natural leadership role of the husband is rooted in biology and sociology, as well as in theology.[22] Biologically the male is built to be the aggressor and the female the receptor. In our society, the male and female are socialized differently so that eventually they play different roles, although this is changing somewhat. The wife's role is further developed as she nurtures her child. Also, he suggests that the husband's provider role logically follows, since the wife is restricted to the child-nurture role. To the above he adds the biblical evidence which supports the male as the leader within the family. (In this connection see Winter's book, *Love and Conflict*, especially chapters two to four.) Some feel that if the wife is submissive to her husband, this is tantamount to saying that the woman is inferior to man. Those who hold to this view, however, would argue that it is not a matter of superiority/inferiority, but a matter of roles to be played.

*Another alternative is that the wife serve as the head of the home.* While this is true in homes where the father is absent, as well as in some homes where the father is present, Winter believes that this is unsound. He suggests that the biological, temperamental, and biblical evidence corroborates the role of the wife in a supportive position within the family. This does not rule out a career for the wife. Nor does it mean that she will not have her areas of expertise. It is worth noting, however, that at least in our society women generally pity men who are submissive to their wives. Furthermore, they do not wholly respect the woman who usurps what they consider the male role.

*Another alternative is that the children rule.* I am not being facetious—I wish that I were. It is not uncommon in some middle-class homes for the children literally to lead their parents about, directly or indirectly. Winter says that filiarchy is the worst possible family-authority pattern. Children are given to parents to be nurtured, guided, and disciplined (instructed). To renege on parental responsibility is to invite disaster. Obviously, as the child matures he is given increasing responsibility so that by late adolescence he has developed into a self-reliant individual.

*Finally, a colleague type of relationship is possible.* In this relationship each exercises leadership in the area of his expertise. Each will do those things that he or she can do best; whether the task is considered a male or a female role by society has no relevance. This equalitarian arrangement appeals to many middle- and upper-class couples. As Nye and Berardo aptly suggest, equalitarian means of equal value, but does not necessarily involve identical responsibility or power. Therefore, one can be equalitarian and yet permit the male to be the leader or head within the family.

Whenever two or more people form a group, someone is bound to emerge as a leader. From the traditional Judeo-Christian perspective this responsibility falls upon the male.

In this chapter we have called attention to several important variables in rational mate selection: endogamous and homogamous factors, theories of mate selection, male and female roles, marriage-career patterns, and various authority structures within the family. All of these are important sociological considerations that have more to do with a wise choice of a mate than either "love" or "sex." We not only have to "love" our spouse, but we must "like" him enough to be "roommates for life!" This is why I contend that the sociological factors are the crucial determinants of marital adjustment and happiness. Let us now give attention to some ways that a couple may test for compatibility.

# 9

# Rational Courtship

*Dating, Courtship, and Physical Intimacy*

Courtship is inevitably preceded by casual dating and steady dating, and followed by engagement. Casual dating refers to dating with no particular goal in mind other than to share an enjoyable period of time together, as a single couple or with a group at some participatory or spectator event. The main goal seems to be to have companionship or fellowship for an event, rather than going alone.

Steady dating, on the other hand, may or may not be goal oriented. If the young people are in high school, they are probably not looking forward to marriage. In this case steady dating serves as "social insurance"; it guarantees that one will have a person to go with to many social activities. Besides providing a sense of security, it may confer a degree of status in some circles among one's peers. Steady dating may convey to others that one is popular and sought after. Not infrequently young people continue a steady relationship because they do not want the bother of establishing a new relationship—it's the path of least resistance.

Another factor that may keep a couple together is some kind of physical relationship. Often the male continues the relationship primarily because of the physical involvement; whereas, in addition to the physical involvement, the female may continue it because she has given of herself completely to the male, believing all the time that they are "in love." Unfortunately, too often the male, more than the female, will later dissolve the relationship when he meets someone else he "really" loves.

Steady dating among older adolescents or young people, however, is usually goal oriented. The couple decides that they want to get to know each other better, so they agree to go steady. Presumably they have filtered through the endogamous factors mentioned earlier and they wish to explore each other's values. In the case of older youth, therefore, steady dating is goal oriented—"perhaps she or he may be the one I will marry." During this period the individuals begin to become exclusive. Each severs any romantic ties or interests he may have with others of the opposite sex. If one finds himself unwilling to do this, it is doubtful that he is ready to progress further with the courtship.

During courtship, the eventual goal is marriage and, therefore, exclusiveness is essential. Courtship should be a time when the couple seriously considers their values, beliefs, and life-goals. It should be a time of honest sharing, of exploring differences, and of assessing whether indeed they are compatible. Robert O. Blood, Jr., suggests that there are several ways that a couple can test for compatibility. However, before we explore these, I believe it is important to emphasize the dysfunctional or negative effect that physical intimacy has in courtship. Too often couples begin to neck and pet early in their relationship. They become physically involved to such an extent that this becomes the primary activity of their dating. We have been programmed by our peers, by Hollywood, and television to think that this is the essence of dating, courtship, and marriage. *It is not.*

The goal of courtship is to get to know the other individual as a person, not to study anatomy! Bowman makes the point that "petting tends to be cumulative." If we begin by necking "a little bit," the next time we will have to go "a little further." He says, "It is a principle of biology and psychology that with repetition the effect of a stimulus tends, under certain circumstances, to decrease. In order, then, to produce the same effect as at first, the stimulus must be increased."[1] Obviously, if intimacy increases indefinitely it will result in intercourse. Therefore, it seems wise for a couple who are serious about each other to talk things over, enunciating clearly their Christian values, and then arranging for dating activities that will support their values and maintain their respect for one another as persons. A good rule of thumb in dating is not to develop any habits or behavior patterns which will be dysfunctional within marriage. This means that we should avoid practices that are contrary to Christian ethics (exploitive) and would have to be unlearned later in the mutuality of courtship and marriage.

## Testing for Compatibility

During steady dating and courtship there are several things that a couple can do to get to know each other better to ascertain whether or not their marriage would be harmonious and mutually fulfilling. The following ways of testing for compatibility are based upon a list enumerated and discussed by Blood in his book, *Marriage*.[2]

Blood's first suggestion is that a couple *vary their dating* pattern to include not only spectator events, but also ones in which both can participate. By interacting with a group each can learn whether the other is an extrovert or an introvert, whether he is tactful and gracious or ill-mannered and sarcastic, whether he is pleasant to be with, or shy and withdrawn. If dating includes events that are formal and informal, activities that take place in the daytime as well as in the evening, one is bound to learn much more than if one always has solitary dates at spectator events. By varying the dating pattern, one will learn to know the whole person, both his strengths and weaknesses.

Through a variety of activities one can get to know the other's hobbies and interests, which in turn reflect his values. If he likes fishing, hunting, and camping, and she dreads all three because she believes it is wrong to kill wild life, then friction is bound to result. If she likes classical music and enjoys hearing serious topics lectured upon, or enjoys reading a serious book, whereas he prefers contemporary rock and folk music and enjoys watching sports on television, but hates to read, they will find it rather difficult sharing their leisure time together. In addition to being fun, dates during courtship should also be learning experiences.

Another way to get to know what makes him or her tick, is to *discuss extensively* during courtship. By spending time just talking and exploring attitudes about Christian beliefs, the church, leisure time activities, family planning, education, and the like, a couple will sense whether or not they share things in common. Discussion will enable the couple not only to learn areas of differences, but also of mutuality. Often one is surprised to learn that one's partner shares similar interests.

One of the questions that often arises is, "How much should one tell of his past life and previous heterosexual relations?" Unfortunately, there is no pat answer. A good question to ask oneself is, "Why do I want to tell about my past?" If it is something that your spouse would find out later from another source, or something that may cause friction later, then it would be wise to share it. If, however, it merely refers to past girl or boy friends with whom there was no pattern of sexual involvement, it might be best to leave it in the past. If one has been sexually promiscuous, however, this is a different matter, as patterns of behavior are not too easily broken. Sharing in this case may be best, not only because a spouse might learn of it from some other source, but also because it might represent a pattern of behavior which might appear again. The incidence of extramarital sex is definitely higher with those who were actively involved with several partners prior to marriage than it is with those who were uninvolved. Therefore, honesty in this type of situation will help the couple to face a potential problem realistically.

*Problem solving* is something we are confronted with

throughout our lives, and marriage is no exception. During courtship, however, how we solve our problems is very important because it augurs ill or well for the future. If, when the couple is confronted with a conflict of interests (for example, where to go on a date) the girl finds herself continually giving in to the boy's wishes, this does not bode well for the future. If the girl finds that the boy responds to problems and conflicts by shouting and refusing to discuss the issue in a rational manner, this suggests some basic insecurity or immaturity on the part of the male. There will be many facets of life together which are apt to reveal a difference of values, beliefs, or opinions. Therefore, it is imperative that the couple begin to develop positive, constructive techniques of compromise and conciliation.

A fourth experience that will enable one to get to know the kind of person he is dating is to *meet his or her friends*. The old proverbs, "Birds of a feather flock together" and "Tell me who your friends are and I'll tell you what you are like," have a great deal of validity to them. While it is true that we all have acquaintances at work and in the community whose lifestyles are different from ours, it is also true that our intimate friends are usually those of like mind and values. If, on the one hand, he likes her friends and she likes his, this suggests that they probably share somewhat of a common lifestyle. If, on the other hand, she objects to his friends' drinking habits, use of bad language, and the like, this ought not to be passed over lightly.

Sometimes a person has two intimate groups of friends, perhaps a radical, rebellious group and a conforming, conservative group. The question that naturally arises is: Which reference group will win out? Another problem might be that one may have few or no friends. If this should be the case, one should ask why. Could everyone be out of step but him?

Another important factor relating to interaction is: How does he relate to her when he is among his friends? Is he proud of her? Is she jealous and possessive? We can tell a great deal about one another by observing how we interact with our friends.

Besides getting to know each other's friends, we should *visit in one another's homes* and become as thoroughly acquainted with our prospective in-laws as possible. As noted earlier, we are all the products of our environment, as well as of heredity. It only makes good sense, therefore, to visit in his home to meet his parents, the ones who molded him for the past twenty years or so. When you are in the home, do you like what you see there? Is he considerate of the other members of his family? Does she respect her parents? Is the home a relatively happy place, or is it full of conflict, with him being a significant contributor? Is he a Mamma's boy—tied to her apron strings? Is she a "spoiled brat," her every whim met by overindulgent parents? These and many other questions can be answered by visiting in each other's homes, not just once, but many times.

The tragedy of many courtships which are conducted on college campuses or outside of each other's community is that the couple does not interact with each other's family. How on earth can one get a realistic picture of one's prospective mate outside of, and away from, his home base?

But just as tragic are young people who do not ask for,

or ignore, the counsel and approval of their parents. Surely we should be mature enough to realize that our parents know our culture and our basic values better than anyone else, apart from ourselves. Furthermore, since they have the advantage of not "being in love," they can give a rather objective opinion as to the suitability of the match. In addition, having lived through the courtship period and having passed through many other stages in the lifecycle, they have the advantage of hindsight—something one cannot buy. They have observed not only their mistakes in judgment and behavior, but also those made by their peers. Unless one has neurotic parents who feign heart attacks and reject every date brought to the house, while other trusted adult relatives and friends give approval, then their evaluation of one's friend should be welcomed and weighed carefully.

Whether we like it or not, in a very real sense we do "marry the family." The folkways and mores, the values and beliefs, the rituals and behavior patterns of the family are the ones that we internalize and, for the most part, identify with. Even if one later rejects his family culture—it remains a part of him and exerts an influence upon him, even if by negative reaction. Therefore, we should not only know ourselves and our intended spouse, but the prospective family also. They are the ones who will become our children's grandparents, uncles and aunts, and so on. I am not suggesting that we are not individuals in our own right, but that we are a part of, and a product of, an institution, the family. When we marry we assume the positions and the roles of married people which, for the most part, have been defined for us by our family and our society.

Finally, the way one treats his mother and father is generally the way he will treat his spouse. I realize that the roles are changed within marriage—we are equals and not in a parent-child relationship. Nevertheless, we do carry behavior patterns with us into marriage.

A sixth important factor is to *take the time* needed to have a good courtship. It is utter folly to think that one can get to know a person well in two, or even six, months! After all, our parents, our peers, and other primary and secondary groups have been socializing us for a long time. The human personality is a complex organism. Even after several months of dating, at most we have only seen the "tip of the iceberg!" Burgess and Wallin surveyed over a thousand couples. Some had dated for eighteen months, some for up to thirty-five, and some even longer. What they found was that the longer the courtship prior to engagement, the smaller the percentage of broken engagements. As mentioned earlier, Christians view marriage as a lifetime commitment (roommates for life!), therefore it is wise to proceed rationally and carefully. Often an individual who may appear at first to be a Sir Lancelot or a Lady Guinevere turns out to be just one of the "regular cast." Then again, one may find that a certain individual grows increasingly desirable as he learns to know her.

A word of caution about periods of separation during courtship. Sometimes short periods of separation provide excellent testing periods. They give us time to see if our hearts grow fonder for one another, or grow fonder for someone else. The prospect of a long period of separation, however, should not propel us into a premature marriage. Prior to the Second World War, the Korean

War, and during the Vietnam conflict, many took the attitude: "Well, we're in love, and we don't know what tomorrow holds, so let's get some happiness while we can!" Too often what the young people did not realize was that one, two, or more years of separation is a long time. During these periods of separation personalities mature separately, each by unique experiences and, as the postwar divorce rates indicate, many found it difficult to pick up where they left off. Therefore, if one anticipates a long period of separation, it might be best to wait until afterwards to renew the relationship. If the relationship is renewed and continues to develop, then there is ample time to make plans for marriage.

Finally, the question arises: *Should a couple live together* to test for compatibility? Since one cannot simulate marriage, with all of its responsibilities as well as its privileges, it is unwise to live together and engage in premarital sex. It is difficult to honestly know beyond a shadow of a doubt if the marriage will actually take place. Furthermore, if one cannot wait until after marriage to have sexual intercourse, what will he do when his wife is eight months pregnant, or what will she do if he becomes ill for an extended period of time, or what will both do if they are separated for a few months?

Blood suggests that the courtship is the *testing* program and the marriage is the *action* program. They should not be confused. My observation on college campuses is that living together does not necessarily become the tie that binds; instead it often becomes the wedge that divides. In fact, one sexual athlete who lived with a succession of girl friends whom he "really loved," finally chose not to live with the girl he "really, really loved" until after marriage!

From a Christian perspective, cohabitation belongs within the bonds of marriage, not outside. While a number of sociologists and popular writers predict the demise of traditional marriage, Mace and Mace maintain that the evidence does not support their contentions. In America, at any rate, most people still look forward to marriage, although in times of economic recession there is a temporary decline in the marriage rate. Sexual adjustment takes a long time to achieve. It cannot be accomplished by a few premarital experiences in a car, in a motel, or in a home while one's parents are absent. Under such circumstances the couple cannot be at ease, since there is usually fear of detection and fear of pregnancy. The meanings and satisfactions derived from the sexual act depend upon the spiritual and psychological understanding and commitment that the couple bring to it. Such understanding and knowledge takes time. While it is reported by Kinsey and others that those women who engage in premarital sex achieve an orgasm earlier than those who are virgins at marriage, orgasm cannot possibly be equated with satisfaction or sexual adjustment. In fact many would support the premise that in the long run virgins at marriage report the greater marital happiness. I contend, therefore, that for the non-Christian as well as for the Christian, sexual intercourse as an expression of love is best reserved for marriage.

## Predictors of Marital Adjustment

Thus far I have suggested ways of testing for compatibility during courtship. In addition to the above suggestions, it might be profitable to consider W. N. Stephens' predictors of marital adjustment.[3] Just as there are no perfect matches, there is no foolproof way to predict marital adjustment. What Stephens has done, however, is survey the literature to see which variables or predictors were most significant for judging the probability of marital adjustment. He rated them A, B, and C, according to the supporting evidence for each. While we have discussed many of these earlier, I will list them and suggest some important considerations related to each.

## *Class "A" Predictors*

1. *Age at marriage*. Early marriages have the least likelihood of success. By early we mean boys about twenty and girls about eighteen. Marriages which take place earlier than this, in which the bride is pregnant, have added difficulty. Over 50 percent of early marriages end in divorce. Stephens says, "The general trend across the studies is: up to the late twenties at least, the older you are, the better your chances."

2. *Length of acquaintanceship*. Generally speaking, the longer the courtship the better you will know one another and the greater your chances will be for success—a year is minimal. Blood and Stephens suggest that a long engagement is better than a short one. My own feeling is that long engagements place an undue emotional strain upon a couple. Six months to a year is a reasonable time. Most couples find that when they begin to prepare for the wedding, they need every bit of that time to make all the necessary arrangements.

3. *Premarital pregnancy*. Stephens advises, "Don't let it happen to you." What more need we say? While no one would deny the reality of the sex drive and the desire

for intimacy, the self-discipline and self-denial will be amply rewarded within marriage and by the mutual respect the couple will feel for each other.

4. *Religiosity*. The poorest marriage risk is an atheist—probably because he has dethroned God and enthroned himself. He submits to no one. When you are "god," you "don't have to take anything from anyone!" Extreme feelings of independence militate against a cooperative venture of any kind, especially marriage. Those who profess a faith and are actively involved in a church have the highest rate of marital stability when—measured by the lowest frequency of divorce. Likewise, those who are married by a clergyman, usually within a church setting, have a better chance than those who elope or are married by a justice of the peace. The rational planning necessary for a formal wedding, even a small one, is likely related to rationality and considerateness in other areas. Unconsciously, the formal wedding which involves family, church, and community is one way we acknowledge that the new family cannot exist in a vacuum, but is related to a kin network and the larger community.

5. *Similarity of faith*. All of the nine studies reviewed agreed that marriages in which both spouses share the same faith have the best chance for success. I might add that when parents urge their children to marry within their own faith—Christians marrying Christians—they are not being bigoted or prejudiced. They are merely recommending what sociologists seem to confirm; namely, that when two Christians can share their faith through a common denominational affiliation, their faith can be nurtured and grow, and they can also find an

outlet for service to Christ. Merely marrying a person of similar faith (Protestant marrying Protestant), however, is not enough. Care must be taken to select one who shares the same type of commitment. As I mentioned earlier, there is a significant difference between a biblically oriented evangelical and a nominal member of one of the many denominations.

6. *Social class.* The poor and men who travel a great deal (salesmen, truck drivers, and the like) are not good marriage risks. Generally speaking, men marry within their own class or marry downward, while women marry men within their own class, or upward. Fourteen studies, Stephens says, correlate social class with marital adjustment, while two find no correlation. It seems logical, therefore, that if a man marries someone in a higher class than his, he will probably experience a strain socially and economically. If he marries across or down, this strain will more likely be avoided. Two studies report that a rich partner marrying a poor one could be a negative factor.

## *Class "B" Predictors*

1. *Level of education.* When marital adjustment tests and ratings were used, there did not seem to be any agreement that level of education correlated with marital adjustment. When they examined the correlation between divorce and education, however, eight studies found that the greater the years of schooling, the lower the divorce rate. One study, however, showed that those with graduate education (beyond the BA) showed a slightly higher divorce rate than those with only the baccalaureate.

2. *Previous divorce.* Those who have been divorced are more likely to divorce again. Two studies reveal that previously divorced men are poorer risks than previously divorced women. The important questions to raise are: What were the reasons for the divorce? and What insights were gained from the previous marriage?

While the New Testament holds up the ideal of the permanence of marriage, most Protestant denominations permit divorce under some conditions. Adultery is the most common.

3. *Divorced parents.* Generally speaking, those whose parents were divorced score lower on marital adjustment tests. Grooms seem to be more affected by parental divorce than brides. Probably children who experience divorce, as well as those who are raised in conflict-ridden, legally intact families, acquire behavior patterns and attitudes which are dysfunctional to establishing a harmonious relationship. Admittedly, few families have not had serious problems of one kind or another sometime during the family life-cycle. While we cannot select our parents, as young people we can strive to overcome those aspects of our family experience which we deem unfavorable. No one wins when we keep projecting blame upon our parents for our failings and shortcomings. As young adults, with God's help, we can become new creations in Christ Jesus.

4. *Place of residence.* Stephens says, "Live in the country or in a small town; don't live in the city." One of the reasons is that life in the city generally includes a greater degree of anonymity and impersonality. Small towns and rural areas often are more neighborly. However, sometimes we cannot choose where we will

live, since our profession, work skill, or the firm that employs us may dictate this. Wherever we live, if we will affiliate with an active church that is able to provide Christian fellowship, this will help integrate us into a group and give us a sense of belonging.

5. *Parent's approval.* Four studies all agreed that it is best to get parental approval *before* you decide to get married. "Either the old folks really know something, or parental objections generate a self-fulfilling prophecy."

6. *Sociability.* Apparently couples who are joiners and interact with others score higher on adjustment tests. Whether or not you share similar leisure time interests and values is worth checking out.

## Class "C" Predictors

1. *Difference in age.* It appears that too large a difference in age is not desirable. If the groom is much older or much younger this could be a negative factor. Five years or more is probably too much. Obviously the age difference is more significant when one is young, than when both are past the middle years.

2. *Brothers and sisters.* The effect on marital adjustment is not conclusive. It does seem logical to assume, however, that someone who is reared with siblings of the opposite sex will have had more experience of a pragmatic nature which should aid in adjustment. So much depends on how much interaction, openness, and discussion took place in the home. It is believed by some that being an only child could be a negative factor, but this again depends upon whether or not he was reared by overindulgent or negligent parents. Also, an only child usually has friends who provide the same, or even better,

interaction than do siblings.

3. *Relationship with parents.* Two studies reveal that children who had conflict with their parents scored lower on marital adjustment tests. Apparently conflict patterns that one acquires in the family persist in marriage. With earnest effort, however, these patterns can be broken.

4. *Relationship before marriage.* Generally speaking, a courtship that is filled with stormy conflict and unresolved problems is a bad sign. If the courtship is a relatively harmonious one in which the couple give evidence that they can communicate and resolve differences amiably, their marriage will probably be a success. It is important to emphasize that a strife-torn courtship is not likely to improve after marriage. It usually gets worse unless there are some dramatic changes in attitudes on the part of one or both individuals.

5. *Mental health.* Good mental health means healthy, mature personalities. Dr. Jack Dominian, a psychiatrist, believes that personality traits are the most important factors in marital adjustment.[4] While I would agree that they are of vital importance, they are intrinsically related to sociological conditions that affect our mental health. Therefore it is not a case of either/or, but both/and.

By way of conclusion, I believe that the experience of courtship can be a profitable experience in many ways, for it is a time when two people who believe they are in love can "test" to see if they are indeed compatible. While some would say that engagement is the time when a couple should get to know one another in depth, I believe that compatibility testing should be done *prior* to engagement. Differences and problems will not disappear. They will persist and become magnified unless they are resolved. Therefore, serious consideration ought to be given to the suggested "tests for compatibility" and the "predictors of marital adjustment."

If courtship is to be a time when we get to know our prospective spouse, physical intimacies ought to be played down. While some affectional display undoubtedly has its place, excessive necking and petting may assume too large a place and blind one to the sociological factors that are the most crucial consideration within courtship.

# 10

## Summary and Conclusion

My thesis has been that merely loving someone, or feeling a sexual attraction for him, is not sufficient reason for selecting him for a marriage partner. Romantic love, which is largely based upon physical attraction, emotional appeal, and fantasy, is a dangerous concept which has been foisted upon American youth by Hollywood, the mass media, and the fertile imagination of various writers. There are always those around telling us that Cinderella romances are possible, despite the fact that in real life they seldom occur. If they do take place, divorce—due to incompatibility based upon divergent social backgrounds, conflicting values, and variant interests—is likely to result. Romantic love narrows our perception. It blinds us from considering essential sociological factors important to rational mate selection.

Furthermore, I have contended that as Christians we ought to love everyone, including those of the opposite sex. Just as God's self-giving love is not altered by our response to His love, our love must be extended to all mankind. We are commanded by Christ to "love our neighbor as we love ourselves." Since this is so, mate selection must be based upon more than love, it must be based upon sociological factors of "likeness." From among those we love, there are those we "like"; those who share similar values, beliefs, and goals. It only seems logical that we should select a prospective mate from among those we like.

When dating and courting, we should minimize the physical expressions of affection. Most societies prior to this century have insisted that any physical demonstration of affection, such as necking and petting, belongs in marriage. In fact, in many parts of the world marriages were arranged by the parents, with the children's consent, but physical intimacies prior to marriage were not condoned. If we are to have a courtship that is rational, physical affection cannot be permitted to dominate the relationship. Since affection is cumulative, it takes an increasingly larger amount to be satisfied. This often leads to premarital sex, which not only runs counter to Christian principles, but too often introduces an element of exploitation, distrust, guilt, and loss of self-respect, as well as respect for the other person.

Furthermore, the fact that two people "fit together" physically does not constitute the kind of total compatibility needed within marriage. Sexual compatibility, per se, is not a sufficient reason to marry. God, in His wisdom, has created us so that virtually any two people can join together in physical union. The vagina can expand to accommodate any penis. Therefore, "plumbing" is not a factor in mate selection!

The crucial elements in mate selection are sociological factors such as religion, socioeconomic class, race, ethnicity, and the definition of various familial values and roles. Equally important are psychological or homogamous factors such as temperament, education, social attitudes, values, and personality. If we court one long enough to get to know him well, using the various tests for compatibility, and then find that we are suited to one another, we are ready to think about marriage.

One aspect of the courtship that needs to be reintroduced is that of visiting and interacting with his or her family in their home. Rational, realistic courtship faces the facts. Each of us grew up within a specific family and community culture that helped mold us into what we are today. Our values, beliefs, and attitudes were absorbed within our families. Therefore, the sensible thing to do is to get to know each other's family. Only in this way can one see his prospective spouse within a social context. The way one interacts there will probably be the way he will interact when he is married. One cannot live in the artificial state of romantic courtship forever. When you are in his or her home, do you like what you see? Do your would-be in-laws approve of you? Do your parents and siblings approve of him or her?

Parental approval is very important because parents are not emotionally involved. This means that they can be more objective and analytical. They have the advantage of having lived much longer than youth. They tend to place the emphasis on rational, sociological, and personality factors rather than on emotional considerations. They also see the broader implications of religion. For them religion is not only a system of doctrinal beliefs, it also includes a specific "way of life."

If we find that our parents are willing to give us their blessing, then we can begin to make preparations for the wedding. This usually takes more time than most couples realize. A wedding is not only a private affair. In a real sense it is a public affair. Not only are our nuclear and extended families involved, but also our friends, our church, and our community. In addition, society at large has a stake in establishing new families. None of us stands alone. We are the product of the total interaction we have had with other human beings. They have given of themselves to us, and we in turn have made a contribution to their lives.

Therefore, when we plan our wedding, whether it is a small home ceremony or a large church affair, we should give as many friends as we can an opportunity to share in the happy occasion. Both parents and families should be involved because we are the fruit of their love. We are their children, and although we relate to them on an adult level now, they are still our parents. Also, our friends inside and outside of our extended families and churches have an interest in us. As members of the body of Jesus Christ, we encourage one another and support each other with prayer.

Usually the pastor officiating at the wedding ceremony will want to speak to the prospective bride and groom. He will probably share with them some insights about marriage that will be helpful to those entering into a new relationship. He will also want the couple to share with him their faith, their hopes, and their concerns.

One thing the couple ought to do is read the wedding ceremony very carefully together. Each will notice that he is really "signing a diffused contract." That is, when one gives his word to love, honor, and forgive he has no way of anticipating how and under what circumstances he will be called upon to do so. Nonetheless he is making a commitment to stay with his spouse through good times and bad, in sickness as well as in health, and during times of poverty as well as affluence. This is an important commitment. He is admitting that he is not expecting perfection of his partner—the going will probably be rough at times. The married experience will probably not be one steady climb, free of conflict or problems. There will be plateaus, and even reversals at times, but each is giving his word to "hang in there!" So, read the ceremony over, discuss it, and pray about it.

Now while I said earlier that love and sex are not enough—neither one is a sufficient reason for mate selection, nor enough to build a marriage upon—once one is married, love (*eros*, as well as *philia* and *agape*) and sexual communion are very important elements in a successful marriage. Love, especially *agape* love, the self-giving kind, is crucial. Each must be willing to give 100 percent, not merely 50 percent, to make the marriage work. In a successful marriage, one must think about responsibilities and duties, more than about rights and privileges. *Agape* love will enable us to support and sustain the marriage relationship, even when we do not think our spouse deserves our support. *Agape* love is the ideal type of love that we should strive to express, for by doing so we will be following in the steps of Christ, and

## Summary and Conclusion/139

we will be strengthening the marriage relationship.

One of the expressions of *agape* and erotic love is communicated through sexual intercourse. Before I discuss this, however, let me answer a couple of criticisms of premarital self-control which have a bearing upon sex within marriage. Some critics of the single sex standard of morality set up strawmen. We often hear some say that if you tell young people that sexual intercourse is a sin before marriage, this will inhibit the free expression of sexual love within marriage. I fail to see the logic in this kind of reasoning. The Christian ethic does not say that marital sex is a sin, but that premarital sex is a sin. We have maintained all along that sex is a beautiful and good thing within marriage where it belongs.

Another criticism lodged is that parents say to their daughters, "Don't give in to the sexual advances of men, because if you do they will not want to marry you." This is suggesting, so the argument goes, that the woman is "buying the man"—she is nothing more than a paid prostitute. While I have heard this argument, this is not an argument that Christian parents use. The Christian girl is not motivated by the fear that no one will marry her if she is not a virgin. But rather she is motivated by love for others, respect for self, and obedience to Jesus Christ. If we are to love ourselves, we must be able to respect ourselves. The woman who uses sex for whatever reason cannot truly respect herself. Nor is she respecting her fiancé if she encourages or allows herself to be used. The same is doubly true for the young man. How can one respect himself if he *uses* or *exploits* his fiancée?

Premarital self-control in no way will inhibit sexual enjoyment and fulfillment within marriage. Quite the contrary; it will enhance it and make it more meaningful. As noted earlier, intercourse becomes one of the signs of love by which we communicate our affection. All things being equal, it is one of the most intimate acts of communion we can share in marriage. Paul recognized this when he wrote to the Christians at Corinth and urged them to share regularly in the act of sexual love. He taught that in marriage the two become one and that each belongs to the other.

J. Richard Udry makes the point that while sex is a mutual experience, husbands and wives view it differently. Women tend to view marriage more from the perspective of the total relationship than men do. Men seem to put a greater value upon sexual intimacy, per se. If the wife denies her husband sexual intercourse, this colors his valuation of the total married relationship. While women value sexual love, they do not necessarily give it the same priority. Marriage partners need to reckon with the differential in perspectives and needs, and express their love in those ways that satisfy their spouses best.[1]

Many contemporary biologists and sociologists believe that the sex drive is basically learned. They maintain that both young women, as well as young men, have similar needs and that one's sexual appetite will vary just as other individual needs vary. It is important for both husbands and wives to be sensitive to each other's needs.

While I began by stating that "love and sex are not enough," I conclude by saying that within the bonds of marriage, love and sex are integral and vital elements of a successful marriage.

# APPENDIX

## Mating in the Faith

*An Exploratory Mennonite
Perspective by Levi Miller*

As teenagers, my brothers and I attended sessions of Conservative Mennonite Bible School which were held in our community. Ostensibly, young people from all over the United States came to study the Scriptures, to learn some Greek alphabet, and to sing rousing numbers in a huge a cappella chorus. But the "hidden cur-

---

There is a growing awareness among young people, as well as among parents and church leaders, that something as important as mate selection should not be left to chance, nor should it be based solely upon romantic love. If one is to be faithful to the Lord through his Christian community (denomination), he must have the opportunity to meet friends of the opposite sex who share a similar faith and commitment to Christ.

This is not something the individual or his family can do by themselves. They need the assistance of those in the church who program youth activities on the local, state, and national levels. By providing opportunities for its youth to fellowship and serve, a church is not only providing opportunity for Christian growth, it is also providing a pool of eligibles from which its youth may select a lifelong partner.

The article in this appendix, "Mating in the Faith" (*Gospel Herald*, August 31, 1976), illustrates that Mennonites are raising the question of their responsibility to their youth. It is not sufficient to say, "Love and sex are not enough." We must also provide opportunity for our youth to meet those with similar values and beliefs. By doing so, we are not only providing for the strengthening of the body of Christ, but we are also providing a sound faith upon which a marriage may be built.—*Charles P. De Santo.*

## 142/Love and Sex Are Not Enough

riculum" included cold evenings—"All shod with steel, we hiss'd across the polish'd ice." A purpose of many of the young people—and, I believe, the parents and administration—was mating.

The issue was raised at the conference sessions which our family would attend. One evening was given to discuss and promote the winter Bible school. The speaker would mention the merits of the school, one of which would come under the general heading of "fellowship." He said that the school was sometimes called a "match factory." Everyone would smile, such as people do when someone speaks the truth. We were told the importance of finding suitable life companions. The school had helped.

If this discussion needs a hero, I nominate that speaker, for he made explicit a basic function of any people who are concerned about passing on a way of life, a faith. He and his audience understood the need to mate within the faith. Or, in negative terms, they avoided being "unequally yoked."

I remembered this speaker recently when I read a book on anthropology and religion. John Westerhoff III and Gwen Kennedy Neville in *Generation to Generation* (Pilgrim Press, 1974) use some of the learnings of anthropology in religious education to ask some of the basic ways in which a society passes on a way of life, its religion. Gwen Kennedy Neville says that two basic requirements of any society are, first, to find suitable marriage partners for the young people, and second, to provide ways to teach the offspring from these unions the faith or way of life (p. 55).

It strikes me that we have spent a large amount of time

and energy on the second need, teaching the faith to the young, but we have not given much conscious effort to the first, finding appropriate mates for the young. Only 18 percent of Mennonite teenagers answered "yes" to the question "Do you think it is important that a person marry a member of his own denomination rather than someone from another background?" (Kauffman and Harder, *Anabaptists Four Centuries Later*, Herald Press, 1975, p. 172.)

Somehow, it seems incongruous that at the very time that we have gained a purer Anabaptist understanding of the church, we should be moving toward an indiscriminate view of socialization. We are becoming a schizophrenic people. Theologically, we want to be an Anabaptist Adonis, but socially we are panting after a promiscuous Venus. Young people marry one another based on romantic love, sometimes one partner not aware of the church's commitment to peace, community, sharing, nonresistance, and service.

The problem is related to our privatization of courting and marriage. For example, in our congregation are several young persons whose biological parents are not members of the church. It would be naive to assume that their future life in the kingdom (as we understand it) does not depend, in many ways, on their finding appropriate mates in the faith, if they choose to marry. Yet, as a congregation we make few conscious efforts to bring them into contact with other Mennonite young people, especially those who do not attend a church college.

A star-crossed Romeo and Juliet are more tuned to our sensibilities than an aged Tobit sending his son to meet the young Sarah. We want our children to marry Christians, we would say, if asked, but we are reluctant to become involved in the process. Love is a private affair.

But, of course, I'm overstating, you say. Perhaps. I spent two terms in the organized voluntary service program of the church and on both occasions met a number of young people who, among other goals of service, were looking for mates. At the time, I felt that goal was at its best humorous and at its worst a perversion of the goals of the program. Today, I see a third possibility. I admire the perception of these young people, for voluntary service has served the holy function of bringing together young people with similar faith commitments. What better place to discover a life companion than among people who share your commitment to serve God and fellow humans here on earth. This is not to say that mating should be a primary goal of VS; neither, however, should it be discouraged.

Because, to my knowledge, this subject has had little written discussion during my married years, what I suggest should be considered exploratory. However, in oral discussions, it has raised considerable interest so that some possibilities may be offered. I will list several.

First, to the extent that we believe that a believers' church (Mennonites, Brethren, Quakers) has a unique vision and way of life for our times, we need to teach and preach the importance of marrying within the faith. I would be disappointed if my son or daughter would marry outside the faith. I say this, knowing that if parents of any other religion, take their faith seriously, they would feel the same about their children.

People who do not take their faith identity seriously, can, naturally, be expected to mate for status, wealth,

*Mating in the Faith*/145

good looks, sex, or friendship. But for us these elements are secondary to our understanding of a biblical faith commitment. There are good reasons why the Old Testament Hebrew community was constantly warned against marrying outside of their own people.

I must add here that if a person from another faith or cultural background comes into the faith and marries, then we no longer have a mixed marriage; indeed, that is what a believers' church is all about. But this clarification does not negate the need for the basic teaching: Persons who hold a belief in the defenseless gospel of Jesus Christ should consciously be taught to mate with persons holding a common faith commitment.

Second, we might begin to deprivatize mate selection. It is the business of the community of faith who persons will live with for the rest of their lives. Indeed, if the climate of love is present (and the teaching is there, as it presently isn't), a young person will seek out the counsel of brothers and sisters in the faith in finding an appropriate mate. I say this without trying to idealize matchmakers, dowries, and the ancient marriage by purchase (e.g., Genesis 31:15). But the traditional involvement of parents and the religious community in mate selection could be a healthy corrective to private affairs.

Nor does community involvement preclude the sexual delight which often surprises people in mating. The Song of Songs, that hymn of the wonders of sexual love, comes from a time when mating was done in the style of Isaac and Rebekah rather than in the private style of our two lonely heroes in *Love Story* of a few years ago.

Third, we need to encourage and support those settings where mating can naturally take place. For example, the church colleges and high schools, the church camps and retreat centers, and youth conventions serve the vital function of bringing together young people who will later provide church leadership and homes for future generations. (For a well-documented account of how one such institution, a retreat center, has served the Southern Presbyterians, see chapter 3 of *Generation to Generation*.)

Again, there is encouragement here. When the conference youth secretaries became tired several years ago and canceled the churchwide youth convention, they were surprised by the firm but gentle rebuke they got from parents and young people at the General Assembly the following year (1975). The concern was natural and holy. The young felt a mating urge and the parents (especially those in outlying and isolated areas) wanted that urge to be taken care of within the faith. This was a strong affirmation of the church.

I began this discussion with a hero; I will end with a heroine. A young woman who grew up in a different communion came to a kind of commitment love to my brother. Over a period of years, she came to know and appreciate our church's faith, life, and rituals, as well as our family's customs, gatherings, and foods.

I would be arrogant if I would not mention that we also benefited from her Presbyterian understandings and her suburban Philadelphia culture. But ultimately a decision had to be made, and in her late twenties, she requested a believer's baptism and has become a member of the family of faith known as Mennonites. She is my sister, a kind of twentieth-century Ruth.

# NOTES

## *Prologue*

1. 1 Corinthians 13:4-8a.
2. 1 John 4:19.
3. 1 John 4:20, 21; Matthew 5:43-48; Luke 10:25 ff.
4. Mark 12:31.

## *Chapter 1: Christians in a Pluralistic Society*

1. In order to avoid needless repetition of "he or she," the terms "he," "him," and "his" are employed throughout the book to refer to both male and female.
2. 1 Corinthians 6:19, 20.
3. John 14:6.
4. 2 Corinthians 6:14.

## *Chapter 2: The Relevance of Christian Faith to Life and Marriage*

1. Mark 12:29-31.
2. Isaiah 6:5.
3. Luke 5:8.
4. John 3:16; Luke 24:45-48; Acts 13:38; Ephesians 1:7.
5. 2 Corinthians 5:17-21; Mark 2:1-12.
6. Ephesians 2:8, 9; 4:32; Matthew 18:21 ff.
7. Romans 12:3; 1 Corinthians 4:7.
8. Matthew 7:24-27.
9. 2 Corinthians 6:14.
10. Mark 10:2-12.
11. 1 Corinthians 13:4-8a.
12. Romans 12:3 ff.; Ephesians 5:21.
13. 1 Peter 3:1-7; James 5:13-16.
14. Ephesians 4:26; Luke 17:3, 4.
15. 1 Corinthians 7:3-5; Ephesians 5:21-33.
16. Ephesians 5:21 ff.; Colossians 3:18, 19.
17. Matthew 16:17, 18; Hebrews 10:25; Galatians 5:13; 1 Corinthians 15:58.

## *Chapter 3: The Importance of Family Background*

1. Ezekiel 18:2.
2. John 3:1 ff.
3. Romans 12:2; 2 Corinthians 5:17.
4. 2 Timothy 1:7; 1 Corinthians 10:13; Philippians 2:12, 13.
5. Romans 12:2, Phillips.

## Chapter 4: The Impact of Youth Culture

1. Alvin Toffler, *Future Shock* (New York: Bantam Books, 1971).
2. Stephen Cotsgrove, *The Science of Society* (London: George Allen & Unwin Ltd., 1972), pp. 209-213. See also Frederick Elkin and Gerald Handel, *The Child and Society: The Process of Socialization* (New York: Random House, 1972), pp. 144-149, and J. Benington, *Culture, Class, and Christian Beliefs* (London: Scripture Union, 1973), pp. 31-41.
3. 1 John 2:15-17; Romans 12:1, 2.

## Chapter 5. The Pros and Cons of Early Marriage

1. John R. Weeks, *Teenage Marriage: A Demographic Analysis* (Westport, Conn.: Greenwood Press, 1976)

## Chapter 6: Love Is Not Enough

1. C. E. B. Cranfield, "Love," in *A Theological Word Book of the Bible*, Alan Richardson, editor (New York: Macmillan, 1951).
2. Robert K. Kelley, *Courtship, Marriage, and the Family*, (New York: Harcourt, Brace, Jovanovich, 1974), p. 214.
3. *Ibid.*
4. *Ibid.*, pp. 13, 14.
5. Robert O. Blood, Jr., *Marriage* (New York: The Free Press, 1969), p.111.
6. Erich Fromm, *The Art of Loving* (New York: Harper & Row, 1956).
7. John 4:7-21.
8. Ralph Linton, *The Study of Man* (Englewood Cliffs, N.J.: Appleton-Century, 1936), p. 175.
9. Blood, *op. cit.*, p. 37.
10. William M. Kephart, *The Family, Society, and the Individual* (New York: Houghton Mifflin, 1972), p. 347.
11. Blood, *op. cit.*, p. 106.
12. *Ibid.*, p. 107.
13. Kelley, *op. cit.*, pp. 222-227.
14. *Ibid.*, pp. 210, 211.
15. John 13:34; 15:12, 17; 1 John 4:11 f.
16. 1 Corinthians 13:4-8, Phillips.
17. C. S. Lewis, *Mere Christianity* (New York: Macmillan, 1960). See chapter six of Book III on "Christian Marriage."

## Chapter 7: Sex Is Not Enough

1. Margaret Mead, *Coming of Age in Samoa* (New York: Mentor, 1949); *Growing Up in New Guinea* (New York: Mentor, 1930).
2. Kephart, *op. cit.*, pp. 146-151; and Stuart A. Queen, and Robert

W. Habenstein, *The Family in Various Cultures* (Philadelphia: Lippincott, 1974), pp. 311 ff.

3. Kephart, *op. cit.*, p. 275.
4. *Ibid.*
5. 1 Corinthians 6:13 ff.
6. Evelyn M. Duval, *Love and the Facts of Life* (New York: Association Press, 1963); Willard Dalrymple, *Sex Is for Real* (New York: McGraw-Hill, 1969); Kenneth L. Jones, et al., *Sex*, (New York: Harper & Row, 1969); Ronald A. Sarno, *Achieving Sexual Maturity* (Paramus, N.J.: Paulist Press, 1969); Herbert J. Miles, *Sexual Understanding Before Marriage* (Grand Rapids: Zondervan, 1972); Elaine C. Pierson, and William V. D'Antonio, *Female and Male* (New York: Lippincott, 1974).
7. Ronald A. Sarno, *Achieving Sexual Maturity* (Paramus, N.J.: Paulist Press, 1969).
8. I. L. Reiss, *Premarital Sexual Standards in America* (New York: The Free Press, 1960). Compare Blood, *op. cit.*, pp. 154 ff.
9. R. F. Hettlinger, "Portrait of the Freshman as a Sexual Being," in *Campus Values*, Charles W. Havice, editor (New York: Scribner's, 1968).
10. Blood *op. cit.*, pp. 156, 157.
11. Kephart, *op. cit.*, pp. 377-380.
12. *Ibid.*, pp. 371-372.
13. 2 Samuel 13:15.
14. Jeremiah 17:9.
15. 1 Corinthians 7:2 ff.
16. 1 Corinthians 6:18.

## Chapter 8: Principles of Mate Selection

1. Nena O'Neill and George O'Neill *Open Marriage* (New York: Avon, 1972).
2. D. W. Truby, "Inter-Racial Marriage," in *All One in Christ: The Biblical View of Race*, P. Sookhdeo, editor (Marshall, Morgan & Scott, 1974), pp. 69-81.
3. F. Ivan Nye, and Felix M. Berardo, *The Family* (New York: Macmillan, 1973), pp. 150 ff.
4. J. Ross Eshleman, *The Family: An Introduction* (Boston: Allyn and Bacon, 1974), pp. 308-312.
5. Nathan Glazer, and Daniel P. Moynihan, *Beyond the Melting Pot* (Cambridge, Mass.: M.I.T. Press, 1970); and M. Novak, *The Rise of the Unmeltable Ethnics* (New York: Macmillan, 1971).
6. B. R. Bugelski, "Assimilation Through Intermarriage," in *Social Forces*, Dec. 1961, pp. 148-153.
7. Will Herberg, *Protestant-Catholic-Jew* (New York: Doubleday, 1960).
8. Kephart, *op. cit.*, pp. 318-329.

# 150/Love and Sex Are Not Enough

9. John Scanzoni, *Sexual Bargaining* (Englewood Cliffs, N.J. Prentice-Hall, 1972).

10. A. I. Gordon, *Inter-marriage* (Boston: Beacon Press, 1964). chapter 4.

11. Blood, *op. cit.*, p. 37.

12. Vernard Eller, *The Sex Manual for Puritans* (New York: Abingdon Press, 1971), p. 50.

13. R. H. Bainton, *What Christianity Says About Sex, Love and Marriage* (New York: Association Press, 1957), pp. 99-102.

14. Nye and Berardo, *op. cit.*, pp. 247-268.

15. J. Bernard, "The Fourth Revolution," in the *Journal of Social Issues*, April 1966, pp. 76-78.

16. David R. Mace, *The Christian Response to the Sexual Revolution* (New York: Abingdon Press, 1970).

17. Galatians 3:28.

18. A. Rossi, "Equality Between the Sexes: An Immodest Proposal," in *Daedalus*, Spring 1964, pp. 607-652.

19. Robert O. Blood, Jr., and D. M. Wolfe, *Husbands and Wives* (New York: The Free Press, 1960), chapter 7, "Understanding and Well-being," pp. 175-220.

20. David R. Mace, *Success in Marriage* (New York: Abingdon Press, 1958).

21. F. Ivan Nye and Felix M. Berardo. *The Family: Its Structure and Interaction* (New York: Macmillan, 1973), pp. 265-268.

22. Gibson Winter. *Love and Conflict* (New York: Doubleday), chapter 3.

### Chapter 9: Rational Courtship

1. Henry A. Bowman. *Marriage for Moderns* (New York: McGraw-Hill, 1974), p. 108.

2. Robert O. Blood, Jr. *Marriage* (New York: Free Press, 1969), chapter 2.

3. William N. Stephens, "Predictors of Marital Adjustment," in *Reflections on Marriage* (New York: Thomas Y. Crowell, 1968), pp. 199-133.

4. Jack Dominian. *Marital Breakdown* (Chicago: Franciscan Herald, 1969), *passim*.

### Chapter 10: Summary and Conclusion

1. Richard J. Udry. *The Social Context of Marriage* (Philadelphia: Lippincott, 1974), pp. 323-325.

# GENERAL INDEX

Absolutes, 19, 23
Acceptance
　in Christ, 32
　self, 32-33
Adolescence, 41, 46-53
　a recent creation, 47
　responsibility of, 41
　sexual development in, 79-80
Affluence, 47, 48, 49
Agape, *see love*
Age
　at marriage, 90, 127
　differences in, 97-98, 131
Alcohol, 98-99, 121
Arranged marriages, 73, 77, 135
Atheism, 21, 23, 128

Basic faith assumptions, 24
Berardo, Felix M., 105, 106, 107, 111, 115
Bernard, Jessie, 107
Bible (Scriptures), 9, 15, 19, 20, 23, 24, 27, 28, 29, 30, 31, 36, 64, 77, 88, 141
Blood, Robert O., 65, 68, 69, 84, 99, 100, 110, 111, 118, 119, 125
Bowman, Henry A., 101, 111, 118
Bugelski, B.R., 95
Bundling, 76
Burgess, Ernest W., 124

Campolo, Anthony, 15
Change
　and marital adjustment, 91
　not necessarily progress, 9
　morality does not, 50-53
　responsibility for, 41-43
　self, not spouse, 91
Character, 100
　formed in home, 40
Christians
　accept Bible as authoritative, 23, 24, 29
　are realistic about human nature, 35
　are reconciled sinners, 27, 32, 35, 41
　believe God exists, 23, 24
　believe in freedom of choice, 28
　believe in racial equality, 28
　believe truth is eternal, 26-27
　belong to Christ, 24, 27
　philosophy of life, 26-27, 30-37
　live in a pluralistic society, 21-29
　love God and neighbor, 18, 24, 135
　must know their faith, 22
　standards not relative, 19, 76
Christianity, 30-37
　as a counterculture, 22
　foundation for marriage, 33-37
　has objective standards, 19, 23, 51
　unique, 23
Church
　and marriage stability, 128
　Christians participate in, 36
　helps integrate into "community," 36, 131
　loss of fellowship in, 103
　the body of Christ, 19, 28, 137
　weddings, 128, 137-138
Civil rights, 28
Coombs, Robert H., 103
Companionship, 110, 112
Compatibility
　as predictor during courtship, 91, 132
　defined, 68
　temporamental, 99
　testing for, 119-126
　　discussion, 120
　　exploring differences, 120
　　living together, 125-126
　　meet friends, 121-122
　　parental approval, 122-123
　　problem solving, 120-121
　　time element, 124
　　vary dating, 119

visit in homes, 122, 136
Communication
  basic between husband and wife, 112
  breakdown in, 56
  necessitates "repentance, forgiveness, and reconciliation," 35-36, 71
  process of renewing, 71
Conflict
  as sign of thinking and growing, 35, 71
  empathic ability and, 72
  expected in courtship, 71, 72, 132
  expected in the home, 42, 55-56
  expected in marriage, 33-34, 35, 37
Conversion, 32, 42
Counseling, 52, 56, 57
Consequences of behavior, 9, 24, 86
  long and short run, 9, 86
Courtship, 116-133
  artificial period, 99
  historical perspective of, 75-77
  irrational, 17
  length of, and stability in marriage, 90, 99, 124-125, 127
  other roles in, 105, 111
  privitization of, 143-144
  rational, 90, 116-133, 136
    based on liking, 73
    faces facts, 136
    minimizes the physical, 135
  recreational role in, 105
  separations during, 124-125
Cultural relativity, 25-27
Cultural universals, 25
Cultural traits, 25, 26-27
  authenticated by Scripture, 27
  vary, 26
Culture
  Christ over, 77-78
  form a consistent pattern, 85
  fun, 49, 50, 58
  molds individuals, 44
  variety in pluralistic society, 22

Dating
  a post World War I phenomenon, 75
  casual, 116
  Christians date Christians, 28-29, 34, 44
  customs change, 77
  differences in, 44, 90
  exclusiveness in, 117
  in "other societies," 75-76
  physical relationship while, 118
  steady, 116-117
  vary activities during, 119
  within same class, 39-40, 95-97, 129
Davis, Keith E., 104
Denominations
  as quasi-ethnic groups, 93
  differences are significant, 94
  marry within, 143
  socialized into, 93
  symbolize a subculture, 43, 93, 94
Discrimination, 28
Divorce, 13, 35, 61, 92, 93, 101
  and early marriages, 61
  interracial marriage and, 92-93
  parent's, 130
  prevalence of, 13
  previous, 130
  same faith and, 93, 128-129
Dominion, Jack, 132
Drescher, John M., 12

Education, 101, 129
Eller, Vernard, 100
Endogamous or sociological factors, 44, 91, 92-97, 104, 115, 117, 136
  ethnicity, 94-95
  race, 92-93
  religion, 93-94
  socioeconomic class, 95-97
Engagements, broken, 83
Ethnicity, 94-95
  commitment to, 95
  differences diminishing, 95
Ethnocentrism, 27-29

## *General Index*/153

Equality of sexes, 59-60
  before God, 36
  not sameness, 108
Extended family, 59, 109

Family
  a source of values, 40
  an institution, 14, 123
  as primary group, 38-39
  authority patterns in the,
    child as head, 114-115
    colleague (equalitarian), 115
    traditional, 113, 115
    wife as head, 114
  confict normal, 42
  marrying the, 123
  rural and urban, 14-15
  unhappiness within, 55
Forgiveness, 27, 31-32, 35-36, 42, 71-72, 88
Fornication, 78, 83
Frame of reference, 24
Freedom, 17, 19, 41, 50
  to choose mate, 72-73
Freud, Sigmund, 70
Fromm, Erich, 65, 70
Fun culture, 19, 49, 50, 58, 105
Future shock, 47

Generation gap, 52
God
  absolute standards of, 19
  commitment to, 33
  first loved us, 18
  forgiveness of, 32, 42, 88
  gave His Son, 63
  grace of, 32, 43, 72, 88
  Holy One, 32
  loves us all the time, 64
  loves us in Christ, 18
  reconciles us in Christ, 32, 42
Glazer, Nathan, 94
Greeley, Andrew M., 93

Harder, Leland, 143
Hedonism, 17, 19, 49, 86

Herberg, Will, 95
Holy Spirit, 33, 43
Homogamous factors, *see mate selection*
Humility, 35

Identity, 30
Independence, extreme, 128
Individualism 17, 19, 23-24, 25, 50
Infatuation, *see love*
In-laws, 122
Interclass marriage, 95-97
Interfaith marriage, 93-94
  church participation and, 103
  conflict in, 94
  divorce rate of, 93
Internalization of beliefs, 93
Interracial marriage, 92-93
  Christian perspective on, 92-93
  divorce rate and, 92

Jesus Christ
  as point of reference, 9, 12
  Christian commitment to, 19
  foundation for courtship and marriage, 29
  grow in grace of, 42
  obedience to, 19
  point of reference in, 9, 12
  the Mediator, 23, 33
  vicarious death of, 32

Kauffman, J. Howard, 143
Kelley, Robert K., 63, 69, 70
Kephart, William M., 68, 76, 84, 87
Kerckhoff, Alan, 104
Kinsey, Alfred C., 126
Kirkpatrick, Clifford, 111

Latent or unintended consequences, 57
Lewis, C. S., 25, 72
Leisure activities, 103, 110
Like, likeness
  basis of mate selection, 67, 68, 73, 115, 135

    in relation to love, 64, 67-68
    physical attraction not sign of, 68
    values and, 64, 134
Love
    agape, 18, 63-64, 71, 73, 138-139
    Christian concept of,
        an ideal, 35
        includes all mankind, 18, 135
        loves neighbor as self, 18, 77-78, 135
        must be demonstrated, 36
        originates with God, 18, 64-65
    definitions of, 68-73
    eros, 63-64, 73, 138, 139
    euphemism for lust, 18, 68
    "falling into," 64, 65
    heterosexual, 64, 68-71
    infatuation, 17, 18, 64-67, 73
    mature,
        a goal, 71
        a state of being, 65
        and the contract, 72-73
        characteristics of, 67-71
        definitions of, 68-71
        includes "like," 67-68
        lifetime commitment, 69, 70, 72-73
        not sole basis for marriage, 18, 19, 67, 73, 91, 134-135, 138
    philia, 63-64, 73, 138
    romantic,
        a pseudo love, 66
        characteristics of, 18, 65-69, 134
        "dangerous," 66, 134
        irrational, 17
        marriage and, 17, 134
        narrows field of perception, 66, 134
        not basis for marriage, 17, 134
        origin of, 65-66
        storge, 63, 69, 73
Lust, 18, 68

Mace, David, R., 107, 111, 126
Mace, Vera, 126

Man
    basic needs unchanged, 51
    can be "born again," 42-43
    created in God's image, 30-32
    egocentric, 31-35
    finite, 31, 71
    needs forgiveness, 32
    not perfect, 32
    redeemed in Christ, 32, 42-43
    sexual being, 18-19
    sinful, 31-32, 35, 41-42, 71
Marriage
    adjustment, predictors of, 126-132
    authority patterns in, 113-115
    change self, not spouse, in, 18, 91
    career patterns of wife in, 111-113
        career, 112-113
        companion, 112
        family plus career, 113
        maternity-homemaker, 112
    choice of partner crucial in, 90, 99
    college, 60
    common faith in, 128-129
    contract and, 72-73
        sacred, 14
        diffused, 138
    early, 54-61
        reasons for not marrying, 59-61
            arrests intellectual development, 59-60, 101
            high divorce rate in, 61
            immaturity and, 56-57, 58, 136
            interferes with career, 59
            limits associations, 60
        reasons for marrying, 55-59
            adult status, 57-58
            companionship, 59
            escape bad home situation, 55-56
            loneliness, 58
            pregnancy, 58-59
            rebellion, 57
            sexual desire, 56
    extramarital sex in, 120
    forgiveness in, 35, 71-72

happiness in, 13
lifetime commitment in, 34-35
love and sex essential in, 140
no perfect, 138
religion and stability in, 128-129
same faith in, 93-94, 128, 141-146
unhappiness in, 12, 13, 55
wife's status in, 105
Mass media, 17, 44, 49, 50, 51, 82, 84
Marrying the family, 123
Masturbation, 79-80
   accidental or habitual, 79
   effect in marriage, 79-80
Mate selection, principles of,
   basic agreement essential, 91, 102
   choice of mate crucial, 90-91, 99
   denomination's duty to aid in, 142-143
   deprivatization of, 145
   endogamous factors in, 92-97, *see endogamous factors*
   homogamous factors in, 97-102, 104
      age, 97, 98, 127, 131
      education, 101, 129
      intelligence, 101, 129
      parallel needs, 99-100
         achievement orientation, 100
         affiliational orientation, 100
      personal habits, 98-99
      personality traits, 99-100
      physical attractiveness, 100-101
      temperament, 99
   no perfect matches in, 126
   theories of, 102-105
      complementary needs, 103-104
      filter, 104
      parental image, 102
      role, 102-103
      value, 103
Mead, Margaret, 75
Mental health, 132
Miller, Levi, 141
Milton, John, 101
Moral law, 25
Moynihan, Daniel P., 94

Neville, Gwen K., 142
New birth, 42
New humanism, 51
New morality, 12, 51
Novack, Michael, 94
Nuclear family, 59, 110
Nye, F. Ivan, 105, 106, 107, 111, 115

Objective standards, 23, 25
O'Neill, W., and G., 91
Oneness, 34-35, 91, 93, 94

Parents
   approval, 52, 122, 123, 131, 136-137
   other's besides, 123
Pastor, 13, 52, 56, 138
Peers, 51-52, 54, 78, 82
   Christian, 52
   pressure of, 51, 60-61
Permissiveness, 49-50, 77
   with affection, 83
   without affection, 83-84
Personality
   and early marriage, 60
   characteristics, 99
   heredity plus social interaction in, 41
   individual responsibility for growth of, 41
   molded in the family, 40
Physical appearance, 100
Physical intimacy, premarital,
   dysfunctional aspects of, 117-118
   is cumulative, 118, 135
   minimize in courtship, 135
Pluralism
   ethnic, 94-95
   in society, 21, 27, 29, 39
   religious, 21
Prayer, 35, 43, 45
Predictors of marital adjustment, 126-132
   class "A," 127-129
   class "B," 129-131
   class "C," 131-132

Prejudice, 27-29
Premarital sex, 74-89
　and self-control, 139-140
　attitudinal differences, 80-82
　as neurotic, 84
　biological factors and, 80-81
　cannot simulate married sex, 87-88
　Christian view of, 74-75, 77-78
　different type of sin, 88
　dysfunctional in marriage, 107
　exploitive nature of, 78, 88, 107, 140
　forgiveness of, 88
　four standards of, 82-84
　　single standard, 82-83, 139
　　double standard, 77, 83
　　permissiveness with affection, 83
　　permissiveness without affection, 83-84
　historical perspective of, 75-77
　latent consequences of, 86
　not preparation for marriage, 87
　peer influence and, 78, 82
　pregnancy and, 127-128
　rationalizations for (and a response), 84-89
　　compatability testing, 87
　　bandwagon, 85-86
　　hedonism, 86
　　"If you love me. . . ," 86-87
　　"other society," 85
　　physiological release, 84-85

Reconciliation, 27, 30, 35, 71
Reference group, 25
Reiss, Ira L., 66, 82
Relativism, 17, 19, 25
Relativity of truth, 25-27
Relativistic secularism, 23-24
Religious faith, threefold division, 22
Religious subculture, 27, 43-44
　socialized into, 43-44
　Christianity as a, 22
Religious surrogates, 21-25
Repentance, 31, 35, 71

Resocialization, 42
Roles
　female and male, 36
　in courtship, 105
　in marriage, 105-111
　female (changing)
　　child care and socialization, 109
　　housekeeping, 110
　　provider, 108-109
　　recreational, 110
　　therapeutic, 111
　male (changing)
　　provider, 105-106
　　socialization of children, 106
　　spiritual leader 93
　male (emerging)
　　recreational, 106
　　sexual intercourse, 107
　　therapeutic, 106-107
Rossi, Alice, 108
Ruben, David, 87

Sanctification, 71
Sarno, Ronald A., 79
Scanzoni, John, 103
Scripture, *see Bible*
Sex *see also premarital sex, sexual intercourse*
　adjustment takes time, 126
　an expression of the "self," 18, 74
　biological factors of, 81-82, 113-114
　biology over reason, 81
　Christianity does not change biology, 80-81
　female/male, 80, 113
　cannot be discussed in a vacuum, 18, 74
　Christian perspective on, 74-75, 77-78, 85
　drive is learned, too, 140
Sexual desire no basis for marriage, 18, 91
Sexual intercourse
　as expression of the "self," 18-19, 75
　belongs in marriage, 88

desire for, not sufficient basis for marriage, 17-19, 51, 134-136
in marriage
differential perception of, 140
means of communication, 36
must be mutual, 107
*one* expression of love, 37, 88, 139
spiritual act, 19, 87-88, 128
symbolic act of communion, 19
vital aspect, 36, 88, 138-140
ordained of God, 36, 74-75
person versus body centered, 107
Sexual revolution, 107
Siblings, 131-132
Socialization, 38-45, 55
a lifetime process, 38-39
begins in infancy, 39, 78
different for each sex, 81-82
family primary agency of, 38, 39, 40, 78
into a subculture, 39, 44
into sexual attitudes, 78
reciprocal interaction in, 41-42
Social class, 20, 39, 44, 95-96, 129
Socioeconomic status, wife assumes husbands, 105-106
Sociological factors, *see endogamous factors*
Social rights, 28
Spock, Benjamin, 109
Stated or manifest goals, 56
Stephens, William N., 126-127
Subculture
Christianity as, 22, 28
denominational, 26, 43-44, 93-94
ethnic, 22, 39, 44, 94-95
family, 39, 43, 44, 136
racial, 22, 44
religious, 22, 43, 44, 93-94
youth, 46-53
Subjectivism, 24

Theism 22
Toffler, Alvin, 47

Udry, J. Richard, 140

Values, 20, 22, 24, 25, 27, 38, 39, 40, 49, 52, 104, 117, 118
American not necessarily Christian, 12, 20
acquired through socialization, 38-40, 136
do not change for the Christian, 51
for all age groups, 52
rural vs urban, 14-15
set by society, 25
vary in each denomination, 22
youth
hedonism, 49-50
individualism, 50
living for present, 49
newness, 50
nowism, 49
Virgin, virginity, 76, 126, 139

Wallin, Paul, 124
Wedding, 137-138
ceremony, 138
pastor, 138
public affair, 137
Westerhoff, J., 142
Winch, Robert F., 92
Winter, Gibson, 113-114
Wolfe, Donald M., 110
Writing essays, 45, 61, 82

Youth culture, *see values*, 46-53

# INDEX OF SCRIPTURE REFERENCES

Gen. 31:15 .................... 145

2 Sam. 13:1-15 ............. 86, 87

Is. 6:5 ......................... 31

Jer. 17:9 ...................... 87

Ezek. 18:21 ................... 41

Mt. 5:43-48 ................... 18
Mt. 7:24-27 ................... 34
Mt. 16:17-18 .................. 36
Mt. 18:21 ff. .................. 32

Mk. 2:1-12 .................... 32
Mk. 10:2-12 ................... 35
Mk. 10:8 ...................... 76
Mk. 12:29-31 .............. 18, 31

Lk. 5:8 ........................ 31
Lk. 10:25 ff. .................. 18
Lk. 17:3-4 .................... 36
Lk. 24:45-48 .................. 32

Jn. 3:1 ff. ..................... 42
Jn. 3:16 ...................... 32
Jn. 13:34 ..................... 70
Jn. 14:6 ...................... 28
Jn. 15:12 .................. 17, 70

Acts 13:38 .................... 32

Rom. 12:1-2 .................. 52
Rom. 12:2 ............. 42, 44, 52
Rom. 12:3 .................... 32
Rom. 12:3 ff. ................. 35

1 Cor. 3:16-17 ................ 78

1 Cor. 4:7 .................... 32
1 Cor. 6:13, ff. ............ 24, 78
1 Cor. 6:18 ................... 88
1 Cor. 6:19-20 ................ 24
1 Cor. 7:2-5 ............... 36, 88
1 Cor. 10:13 .................. 43
1 Cor. 13:4-8 ........ 18, 35, 44, 70
1 Cor. 15:58 .................. 36

2 Cor. 5:17 ................... 42
2 Cor. 5:17-21 ................ 32
2 Cor. 6:14 ............... 28, 34

Gal. 3:28 .................... 108
Gal. 5:13 .................... 36

Eph. 1:7 ..................... 32
Eph. 2:8, 9 .................. 32
Eph. 4:26 .................... 36
Eph. 4:32 .................... 32
Eph. 5:21 ff. ........... 35, 36, 70

Phil. 2:12, 13 ................ 43

Col. 3:18, 19 ................. 36

2 Tim. 1:7 ................... 43

Heb. 10:25 ................... 36

Jas. 5:13-16 ................. 35

1 Pet. 3:1-7 ................. 35

1 Jn. 2:15-17 ................ 52
1 Jn. 4:7-21 ................. 65
1 Jn. 4:11 ff. ................ 70
1 Jn. 4:19 ................... 18
1 Jn. 4:20, 21 ............... 18

**Charles P. De Santo** is professor of sociology and chairman of the Sociology/Anthropology/Social Work department at Lock Haven State College, Lock Haven, Pennsylvania. He received his academic training at Houghton College, Temple University (BS), Louisville Presbyterian Theological Seminary (M Div), Ball State University (MA), and Duke University (PhD).

Before coming to Lock Haven State College, De Santo taught Bible and religion at Maryville College (Tennessee), Sterling College (Kansas), and Wheaton College (Illinois). He taught Hebrew and Old Testament in Wheaton's Graduate School of Religion. He also taught sociology at Huntington College (Indiana) prior to coming to Lock Haven.

In addition to the present volume, he is the author of a

commentary, *The Book of Revelation* (Baker Book House, 1967). He has contributed articles to *His*, *The International Journal of Moral Education*, *The Evangelical Quarterly*, *Interpretation*, *Religion in Life*, and *Eternity*.

He is coeditor of *A Reader in Sociology: Christian Perspectives* (Herald Press, 1980).

Professor De Santo, an ordained minister in the United Presbyterian Church, has spoken on numerous occasions to youth groups, at retreats, and college campuses.

De Santo was born in Philadelphia, Pennsylvania. He is married to the former Norma A. Michener, and they have four children: Stephen, Deborah, Susan, and Timothy.